Here's what students are saying ...

Transforming the IDT and Learning to Parent Yourself Well

"Very helpful and informative course that really puts a name to the monster we deal with. Toni is compassionate, kind, and understanding as well." — Jenny Bennett, July 22, 2017

"Toni is magical. Her ability to draw the real picture of what is going on into manageable concepts is unmatched. She is able to weave connection in an area that otherwise feels isolating and painfully unique. Toni's approach is compassionate, calm and freeing. — Julie Peterson, August 10, 2017

"I experienced multiple "aha" moments while taking this course. I've never analyzed why I get overwhelmed by a project, or to-do list, and have the hardest time trying to decide what to do next, or getting up the steam to tackle any part of the situation. Discovering the option of asking what "I" would really like to do instead, and even giving myself permission to do it — this is something I've never permitted my inner self. I also heavily resonated with the information on making mistakes and how easy it is to become trapped by fears of embarrassment — a huge limitation on my possibilities.

"Toni emphasizes the need for us to be in touch with our bodies. I realized in my life that my brain has commanded my body to follow prescribed courses of action, often completely disregarding my body's discomfort. I'm now learning that paying attention to my body first is the key to breaking down fears and historic resistance to new adventures.

"Taking this course has helped me reframe my past, but more importantly for me now, helps move me forward to challenge limitations and rethink how I live my life. Thanks for the nudges to recreate my life into something more invigorating." — Stephanie Brooks, August 16, 2017

Other books by Toni Rahman

Being In My Body: What You Might Not Have Known About Trauma, Dissociation & The Brain

Boundaries 101: Learning to Recognize, Honor and Communicate Your Personal Limits

Tahóle: The Politics of Love

Self Abuse
&
The Inner Drama Triangle

Transforming the IDT &
Learning to Parent Yourself Well

by

Toni Rahman, LCSW

For more information about this topic, visit https://www.tonirahman.com/course/self-abuse-the-inner-drama-triangle/ and consider enrolling in the course which can be purchased alone or with various bundle options.

Published, printed and distributed in the United States by Open Sesame Publishing.

Columbia, Missouri

For all the women in my family tree past, present and future.

Table of Contents

Foreword

Violence and abuse, regardless of their source, need to be recognized for what they are. When playing out in your own psyche, they can make you feel powerless, confused or overwhelmed. This might look like a relentless barrage of self-criticism, or a sudden, crippling doubt that you have any idea what you are doing. You may be unable to snap out of it or express why. Outside cues might not make sense. You only know that you feel bad and aren't sure how to get back to yourself. This is called an emotional flashback. It is the automatic response of re-living a painful situation from your very early life.

This course is about recognizing and eliminating self-abuse. It demystifies the Drama Triangle, and how it can show up inside our heads (with the different parts of *us* represented by different parts of the triangle). In the course you will gain some tools needed to parent yourself better, and gain a stronger sense of trust in yourself and your own judgment, even when things don't go the way you had hoped or expected.

The course has six modules. Each module is intended to take about a week to complete. I encourage you to take your time with each module, absorbing the information of each one before moving on to the next. If you want, go back and read the material again. Go back and watch the video again, complete the exercises and think about them. If you feel blocked, sleep on it. Talk to somebody else about it. The ideas I'm using can seem complex and nuanced so it will help a lot if you can become really familiar with these terms and concepts. Then you can build on them as we go along.

This workbook version of *Self Abuse & the IDT* is adapted to stand alone as your companion in recovery from early childhood abuse and neglect or as a facilitated course. If you have purchased this book, you are eligible for a discount on the online course. If you enroll in the course, you get the same material, but you also get the embedded links that make viewing videos and online material so much easier.

Sign up to be part of the Self Abuse & The Inner Drama Triangle Facebook Group. Once you are a member you can ask for links to referenced videos and other resources. You may also be able to find these resources by going to YouTube and typing in the name of the video or resource there. Join the Facebook Group here: https://www.facebook.com/groups/1039378412862770/

The intention of this course is to help people better understand and more readily identify emotional flashbacks (in the absence of being able to clearly feel or identify emotions in the way "normal" people do) and internalize a healthy inner guidance system (masculine and feminine) that they didn't experience as children. Trauma therapist and author Toni Rahman gives Coach (Inner Feminine) and Challenger (Inner Masculine) their own distinct voices, questions, and approaches to overcoming the triggers of early relational trauma. These inner voices and resources line up with current attachment and neuroscience research.

Pre-Test:

1) The following are signs of internal or self-abuse:

   A. Tendency to criticize, blame or judge yourself.
   B. Recurring feelings that you can't trust your judgment.
   C. People in your outer life who regularly abuse and disrespect you.
   D. All of the above.

2) (True or False): Flashbacks are only experienced by people who have survived war, rape, assault, or physical violence.

3) The framework that has been used for describing and understanding the chaos of dysfunctional families is called:

   A. The Empowerment Triangle
   B. Sensory Motor Psychotherapy
   C. The Drama Triangle

4) (True or False): The object of the Drama Triangle game is to gain "Victim Status" in order to manipulate others into anticipating and trying to satisfy your needs. In this way, you can gain the care and attention of others without having to take responsibility for knowing or asking for what you want and need.

5) Which is true:

   A. The three players in the Drama Triangle are Victim, Rescuer & Persecutor
   B. The Drama Triangle game has only negative effects on the family, group, or society that plays it.
   C. Abuse can only be inflicted from the outside, from an actual person.
   D. Being willing to ask for what you want and need 100% of the time is the same as asking for what you want and need 100% of the time.
   E. All of the above.

Module 1 - Introduction to the Tools

Tool One: The Drama Triangle

In the field of developmental trauma we have a framework for describing and understanding the chaos of dysfunctional families. It's called the Drama Triangle. In their book, *How to Break Free of the Drama Triangle & Victim Consciousness*, Drs. Barry and Janae Weinhold describe how the Drama Triangle plays out between family members or community members, and in work environments, religion and politics. To add to the chaos, the players of the game continually switch roles, which confuses everyone, and then no one can correct or eliminate the problem, thus cementing the dysfunction into place.

When the various roles of the triangle play out in the mind of a single individual, it can be even more confusing. And since the individual is on his or her own with the problem, the impulse is to deny, hide or conceal it. And without help, the resulting snarl is nearly impossible to untangle.

What's interesting is that when the Drama Triangle plays out in families, it serves a useful role, and fills some important needs. It allows a family's members to connect in the absence of better social and emotional skills. However, the quality of the connection is chaotic, volatile and often abusive. But connection in whatever form is vital, nonetheless.

No matter where it plays out, the person who "wins" the Drama Triangle "game" gets what they want and need without having to ask for it. This is referred to as reaching "Victim Status." Yes. You read that right. In this game, you win by achieving Victim Status. But, as you will quickly understand, playing the Victim gets you nowhere, fast. Luckily, there's another way: Learning to be willing to ask for what you want and need 100% of the time (whether or not you actually ask). This is the key to exiting the Drama Triangle and recovering from early relational trauma.

Before continuing, please watch the online PowerPoint presentation, which will explain the Drama Triangle and how it plays out in our lives: https://www.slideshare.net/marva78/the-drama-triangle

Here is the link again: https://www.slideshare.net/marva78/the-drama-triangle

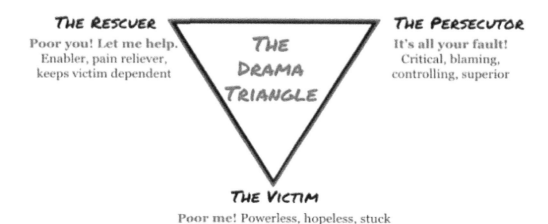

In the Drama Triangle Game, the Rescuer jumps into action as an automatic reflex, fixing things and protecting the Victim, but at the same time keeping the Victim from experiencing real emotional growth or even the fullness life can offer, often fostering unhealthy dependence. Persecutor also jumps in with a lot of noise and energy. Persecutor emerges under particular stressful circumstances, pushing his weight around and saying and doing things that really hurt. Engaging in this game creates so much chaos that it keeps everyone involved at a safe distance from deep feelings and memories of vulnerability and loss associated with early childhood. Ironically, the object of the Drama Triangle game is to gain Victim status, because with Victim status, one is poised to get her needs met without directly asking for them because who can say no to a person who has collapsed into victimhood? Certainly nobody who agrees to play this game. Refusing to play the game, which involves learning new skills, is the only way to really win.

As we move forward in this Workbook, I use the name Tender Vulnerable Part (TVP) instead of Victim. It is difficult for many of us to identify with our tender vulnerable parts, and none of us wants to identify with victimization as a status. It is my hope that using the term TVP will enable you to see this part of yourself with much softer eyes.

Tool Two: The Sacred Inner Marriage (Surrender)

The Sacred Marriage, or Surrender, consists of two characters: Inner Feminine and Inner Masculine. These characters appear in many spiritual, intellectual and esoteric discussions. Every person has both feminine and masculine aspects. For our purposes, I'll break these aspects down as follows.

Inner Feminine

The Inner Feminine is the part of the healthy psyche that works with the Inner Masculine to support an individual in living up to his or her fullest potential. In terms of Surrender, she represents an individual's willingness to _receive_ without resistance or judgment. I'm not talking about willingness to tolerate, or going along to get along. Nor am I talking about passive enjoying (of the "isn't this nice" variety). I'm talking about opening; a conscious, active receiving, which requires the lowering of shields, armor, fear, and expectations. This kind of opening requires consultation with the body and noticing its responses, moment by moment. When we pay attention to the body, it can often tell us the truth better than our conditioned minds can. The body is the premier expert on what you like and don't like. And yes, I'm talking about pleasure, which is something that many of us still have leftover, unexplored suspicions about. With good reason. We will talk more about this in Module 3: Ego Defenses.

> **_Feminine Surrender_** _– Willingness to receive without resistance or judgment; reaching for relief, reaching for more and better, sweetness, pleasure, gratitude: Full receptivity to what nourishes and pleases me._

Inner Feminine is characterized by her unconditional compassion, curiosity and nurture. She provides attunement, encouragement and support. She helps an individual recognize where he or she has inadvertently given power away, and helps set that right. With personal power reestablished, she encourages true independence and healthy interdependence. She offers information to and is supported by the Inner Masculine who is working on an action plan. If we can pause and listen, she says to us, "I see that this is difficult for you."

> Questions Inner Feminine might ask us to help us focus our compassionate attention on ourselves:
>
> > *What's alive in you right now?*
> > *What wants to be met right now?*
> > *What is calling for love right now?*
> > *What has come to ask for help?*
> > *What wants to be touched?*
> > *What wants to be drenched with awareness and attention?*

Inner Feminine is well aware that these sensations and feelings you are grappling with are all parts of you that are longing for love and attention. She lets you feel her presence. Supported by Inner Masculine, she is strong enough to easily withstand the full force of all your emotions. "I'm right here with you," she says. Her voice is soft and gentle. "Take your time. It's safe to be curious about the nuance and information carried by these feelings. You have the support you need. Don't avoid or try to control this. Surrender so that it can flow through you and resolve." And from this place you no longer feel powerless. You are no longer flinging your attention outward; your attention is right back where it belongs.

Inner Masculine

Inner Masculine is the part of the healthy psyche that represents surrender to the soul's clamoring potential; the willingness to take charge of life without guilt. Inner Masculine supports Inner Feminine in staying connected with the soul's deepest intention from which to pursue what is desired.

> **Masculine Surrender** – *Willingness to take charge of my life without guilt or shame; In Charge/In Control, doing, working, applying effort.*

Inner Masculine also asks questions to establish safety and hold the individual accountable, while encouraging learning, action, and next steps.

Questions Inner Masculine might ask in order to establish safety and hold you accountable:
What is your intention in this situation?
What is needed in order to take charge of your life?
What's real here?
Is there something you can do to further your learning and growth here?
In what ways has this unwanted behavior/automatic response actually served you? (working as a way to escape, shutting down emotions, self-criticism, etc.)
How can the energy of this unwanted emotion be discharged safely?
What need does this behavior/attitude/belief fulfill?
In what ways does it need to be honored?
What is it telling you?
How can it be used for good?

Drama Triangle Self-Inventory

On a scale of 1 to 4, please indicate how true these beliefs are with regard to how you think about yourself and others. Place a number in the blank in front of each item that indicates what number is true for you.

Key: 1 = Hardly Ever; 2 = Sometimes; 3 = Frequently; 4 = Almost Always.

_3_ 1. It is my fault when someone gets angry with me.

_2_ 2. Other people's feelings/needs are more important than mine.

_4_ 3. People will think I am too aggressive if I express my feelings/needs directly.

_2_ 4. I worry about how others may respond when I state my feelings or needs.

_3_ 5. I have to walk on eggs so I don't do something that causes people to get angry with me or abandon me.

_4_ 6. I have to give up my needs in my relationships so people will want to be with me.

_4_ 7. I must be perfect so that others will love me and not abandon me.

_4_ 8. I need to rely on others to make important decisions.

_1_ 9. I must hold back when reacting to what others say and do, rather than saying what I believe.

_4_ 10. How I feel about myself depends on other people's opinions of me.

_4_ 11. It's dangerous for me to ask directly for what I want or need from others.

_2_ 12. I avoid assuming a position of responsibility.

_4_ 13. When faced with a problem, I can only think of two conflicting solutions to the problem.

_1_ 14. I need to make sure I meet other people's needs so they will like me and want to be with me.

_4_ 15. It's best to seek out relationships where I can meet the needs of others and make them happy.

★ _3_ 16. If I have to ask for what I want or need from loved ones, they don't love me enough to know what I need.

_4_ 17. I have a difficult time knowing what I want or need.

_1_ 18. I can't let others get too close to me or my life will be consumed by their needs.

_2_ 19. I have difficulty in knowing how I really feel.

_2_ 20. I exaggerate my accomplishments when I meet someone new, so they will like me.

_2_ 21. If people knew who I really am, they would not want to be with me.

_2_ 22. I'm afraid people will find out that I'm not who they think I am.

_1_ 23. I can't ask other people for help, even when I need it because they will think I am too needy.

_1_ 24. I feel controlled by what others expect of me.

_3_ 25. I feel it is really important for me to have the "right answers" or others will think I am stupid.

_2_ 26. I can't admit to a mistake because I am afraid people might reject me if I did.

_1_ 27. I reject offers of help from others, even when I need them.

_4_ 28. I compare myself to others, because I feel either one-up or one-down in relation to them.

_2_ 29. I feel hurt when others don't recognize my accomplishments.

_2_ 30. I don't deserve to be loved by others.

_81_ Total Score

$1 \times 5 = 5$ $3 \times 4 = 12$

$2 \times 10 = 20$ $4 \times 11 = 44$

30
19
11

49
12
20
5
81

Interpretation of Scores:

30-50 = Few beliefs that contribute to the Drama Triangle in your life.
51-80 = Some beliefs that contribute to the Drama Triangle in your life.
81+ = Many beliefs that contribute to the Drama Triangle in your life.

Note: The items you answered as "3 or 4" have the most control over you.

From *How to Break Free of the Drama Triangle & Victim Consciousness* by Barry K. Weinhold and Janae B. Weinhold. 2016.

Inventory for Internal Disequilibrium
●Self-Abuse ● Self-Abandonment ● Self-Neglect

On a scale of 1 to 4, please indicate how true these behaviors are with regard to your internal environment. Place a number in the blank in front of each item that indicates what number is true for you.

Key: 1 = Hardly Ever; 2 = Sometimes; 3 = Frequently; 4 = Almost Always

_2_ 1. Complaining to myself or others
_1_ 2. Disconnecting in whatever ways I can from emotions/needs
_1_ 3. Denying emotions
_4_ 4. Trying to get rid of parts of me (I wish I didn't have to deal with _____.)
_3_ 5. Annoyed with parts or aspects of my physical body
_3_ 6. Refusing to forgive myself for something I did in the past
_4_ 7. Expecting perfection
_4_ 8. Remaining disconnected from the self, the body, or its needs/feelings for more than 1-2 hours
_3_ 9. Being harsh & unrelenting with myself
_3_ 10. Expecting things that aren't realistic from my body
_2_ 11. Aligning with ego defenses over self-connectedness and integrity with the body
_2_ 12. Using credit cards (and not paying them off at the end of the month)
_1_ 13. Doing things for others that I'm not sure I can afford
_2_ 14. Expressing disgust and/or contempt to parts of myself
_2_ 15. Feeling critical or judgmental or blaming others
_1_ 16. Feeling repelled or disgusted by others
_3_ 17. Noticing a repeating refrain that sounds kind of like an explanation to put an issue to rest, but the issue doesn't actually resolve
_3_ 18. Punishing myself for a past mistake

____ Total Score

Interpretation of Scores:
18-30 = Few behaviors that contribute to dis-equilibrium in your inner environment.
31-69 = Some behaviors that contribute to dis-equilibrium in your inner environment.
70+ = Many behaviors that contribute to dis-equilibrium in your inner environment.
Note: The items you answered as "3 or 4" are the behaviors that are most damaging.

The Disorganized Attachment Style Inventory
Barry K Weinhold, Ph.D

Directions: Select the number for each item that best describes your experience.
Key: 1 = Not at all; 2 = Occasionally true; 3 = Usually true; 4 = Most of the time

✗ _3_ 1. I forget what I am saying in the middle of a sentence.
_2_ 2. I get confused when I try to remember any negative experiences from my childhood.
_4_ 3. I suffer from momentary lapses in memory while I am talking to others.
_4_ 4. I remember times when I was frightened by what one of my parents said or did to me.
_4_ 5. When I was growing up one or both of my parents seemed "checked out."
_4_ 6. My parents said or did things to me when I was a child that confused me.
_4_ 7. I tend to manipulate others to get what I want or need from them.
_1_ 8. When I was a child, one of my parents was addicted to alcohol or drugs.
_4_ 9. My parents seemed to enjoy saying or doing things to frighten me.
_4_ 10. I find myself "day dreaming."
_4_ 11. My parents would sometimes make sounds or faces that scared me.
_4_ 12. When I was a child, my parents seemed more interested in their careers or jobs than in me.
_2_ 13. I tend to assume responsibility for others feelings and/or behavior.
_2_ 14. I seek out relationships where I feel needed and attempt to keep things that way.
_3_ 15. I am extremely loyal to others, even when that loyalty is not justified.
★ _4_ 16. I have a high tolerance for inconsistent and mixed messages from others.
_3_ 17. I tend to put the needs of others ahead of mine.
_4_ 18. I tend to value the opinions of others more than my own.
_1_ 19. I feel like a coiled spring inside.
_1_ 20. I enjoy being the boss of other people.
_3_ 21. Important people in my life have abandoned me emotionally or physically.
_2_ 22. When I think about my childhood, I draw a big blank.
_4_ 23. I feel empty and alone.
_4_ 24. I have a hard time defining what I need or want.
_4_ 25. I tend to question the motives of others.
_2_ 26. I have a short fuse when I get frustrated with myself or others.
_2_ 27. I am at my best when I am helping others.
_4_ 28. My thoughts seem to have a life of their own.
_3_ 29. I have big gaps in my memory about my childhood.
_3_ 30. I have trouble paying attention to what others are saying.
_____ Total Score

Interpretation:
If your score was between:
40-60 – Some evidence of disorganized attachment style.
61-90 – Moderate evidence of disorganized attachment style.
91-120 – Strong evidence of disorganized attachment style.

Module 1 Quiz 1:

1) (True or False) Inner Feminine is a part of the psyche that is interested in moving toward fulfillment, pleasure, and what feels nourishing, and delightful to the system.

2) Which is true?
    A. A healthy psyche involves a constant battle between Inner Feminine and Inner Masculine.
    B. Masculine Surrender has to do with willingness to receive without resistance or judgment.
    C. Feminine Surrender has to do with taking charge of life without guilt.
    D. Trust in the self and inner peace result from cooperation and balance between Inner Feminine and Inner Masculine.

3) Which is true?
    A. Conscious, active receiving requires the lowering of shields, armoring, fear and expectations.
    B. The mind knows better than the body about the "truth" of any situation.
    C. Inner Feminine helps us focus on what the other person might be feeling or needing.
    D. Inner Masculine is responsible for punishments and rewards.
    E. A and C

The Drama Triangle and Sacred Inner Marriage: Working Together (Becoming the Parents We Always Wanted)

Regardless of your age or the parents you had, you can learn to better parent yourself. What would it look like if we could feel safe and supported enough to stay calm and present, grounded in a sturdy sense of self, even in the face of change, or something unexpected? What if there was some way that we could access the support of the parents that we didn't have, but so desperately needed? Good parents keep children safe, know that the best learning happens when the child is calm and relaxed, and that making mistakes is an important part of life. Good parents stay connected even when their children are frightened, misbehaving or angry. They have the skills to manage their own fear, anger and disappointment, and model healthy behaviors for their infants and children. Good parents are well supported, mature, and attentive to their children. They notice their behaviors, and are attuned enough to pick up on and tend appropriately to important signals of vulnerability and gently provide the support that is needed. Good parents know that their children develop mastery over their emotions over time, and cannot develop emotionally without the help of the adults around them. Good parents also know that they need not be perfect to be good enough.

What would life be like if we all had parents like that, inside of us?

On the following two pages is a diagram showing the various players of the Drama Triangle Game, and their respective traits, as well as the needs they fill. Pay special attention towards the bottom of each column, where you will be introduced to the Creator, Coach and Challenger. These characters are the healthy alternatives to the players in the Drama Triangle game and are features in what David Emerald calls The Empowerment Dynamic (TED). Also notice how the diagram shows alliances:

The Sacred Marriage between Coach (Inner Feminine) and Challenger (Inner Masculine)
The unhealthy alliance (based on shame) between Tender Vulnerable Part (TVP) and Rescuer

Internal Drama Triangle with Sacred Marriage

Player One	Player Two	Player Three
TVP (Creator) *Powerless, stuck, hopeless.*	*Rescuer (Coach)* *"Poor you! Let me help you." Jumping in to "fix" it.*	*Persecutor (Challenger)* *"It's your fault!" Critical, contempt, superior, controlling, blaming.*
Inner Feelings & Dialogue	*Inner Feelings & Dialogue*	*Inner Feelings & Dialogue*
I'm suffering and I can't do anything about it.	Taking responsibility for things you have NO control over.	All the things you are saying to yourself that are dishonoring you.
They have so much power/I have none.	Making assumptions/Jumping to conclusions in attempts to explain this situation and why I'm in it:	You <u>should</u> be able to figure this out.
I've been thrown away.		You're just <u>too</u> sensitive.
I am not valued.	I must be worthless.	Remember that <u>controlling behavior</u> can also be silent, and be just as destabilizing.
My voice isn't heard.	It's probably my fault.	
TERROR	I must have done something to deserve this.	
TOTALLY HELPLESS	If I can figure out what I did wrong, maybe I can fix this.	Cutting you out of the conversation
FRUSTRATION	Listen more carefully?	Silent Treatment
NOBODY could possibly understand what I'm going through.	Smile bigger?	☆ Not responding to your attempts to connect.
CONFUSION (not able to connect logical cause and effect).	Be nicer?	
	Don't cry so much?	
Outrage! "What the Bloody Hell?"	Don't have needs?	
Betrayal	If that doesn't work:	
Rage	Throw a tantrum?	
Overwhelm	Shift attention to the pain of others, and then help them (shift into Rescuer mode).	
I need help regulating my emotions. My nervous system isn't developed enough to do that yet.		

I need the help of an attuned, adult brain to develop my ability to regulate my emotions.		
Needs served	**Needs served**	**Needs served**
TVP (Tender Vulnerable Part): serves the important role of helping us know when something is wrong. She/He does this in whatever way she/he can.	**RESCUER:** serves the important need of feeling like you have some control in your life.	**PERSECUTOR:** serves the important need of discharging the energy of emotions, when you don't know how else to do it.
Healthy Alternative	**Healthy Alternative**	**Healthy Alternative**
CREATOR: "What do I want?" Receptivity to positive change, incremental improvement. "Does this feel acceptable to me?"	**COACH:** Attunement, sensitivity to emotions, ability to read and utilize emotions.	**CHALLENGER:** Re-establishing Safety, accountability, learning, growth, action, next steps.

	Sacred Marriage (based on empowerment): Getting off the Drama Triangle helps us better understand and eliminate abuse while supporting:	
	Feminine Surrender (Divine Bliss) Willingness to receive what I want without resistance or judgment.	**Masculine Surrender** (Servant Leader) Willingness to take charge of life without guilt or shame (willingness to ask for what I want and need). Secret to getting off the Drama Triangle/Critical Skill for completing INDIVIDUATION.
	UNHEALTHY BOND - based on shame. TVP agrees to remain dependent/powerless to honor the Rescuer (or so as to not disturb or "trouble" Rescuer). Rescuer requires TVP to remain weak so that she can thrive.	

Emotional Flashback

In order to better understand what's being presented here, let's revisit the emotional flashback. Adults with unresolved early relational trauma can, in times of extreme stress, or without apparent provocation, regress to an earlier, unresolved, emotionally-traumatic time in their lives. They might feel trapped in a similar sense of powerlessness or overwhelm, as if they were very young and dependent on others for all their needs. Even though they are now adults, they feel powerless, and their thoughts can cycle between terror, rage, overwhelm and confusion. Or they can merely cycle between criticism, judgment and self-doubt.

This is what we refer to as an emotional flashback. Regardless of the intensity or the topic, if you are caught in a loop of nonproductive thinking, are having trouble making important connections between cause and effect, or feel powerless in the face of overwhelming circumstances, you are probably experiencing emotional flashbacks. The good news is that there is help, and it is closer than you think.

It always helps to remind yourself that the feelings you have during an emotional flashback (although intense, confusing and unpleasant) are temporary. That doesn't mean you should ignore them (as if you could). It means that as long as you are in the flashback, your feelings require your attention, compassion and care. And there are things you can do to avoid making it worse. If you suspect you're currently in a flashback or have recently made your way back from one, this course is offered as a "life ring." I hope you can and will hold on. If you do, you'll find your way back to safety. Looking back after it's over, you will be grounded in your own resources, and have a reliable framework of understanding that you can return to again and again. With it, you'll be able to more and more quickly exit emotional flashbacks in the future, and each time you will be wiser and stronger than you were before you entered.

Getting triggered into emotional flashbacks frequently or staying triggered for periods of time is a sign of Complex Post Traumatic Stress Disorder (CPTSD). There has been a great deal of research done on this topic, and it affects more people than you might imagine. Despite the fact that they feel miserable and crippling, flashbacks can be used as unique opportunities to gain vital information to help you heal your childhood wounds. These are not just arbitrary occurrences. And they're certainly not a form of punishment or just plain bad luck, either. You are not a victim of circumstances. And learning more about the Drama Triangle will give you a language to turn your Inner Persecutor into an Inner Challenger and your Inner Rescuer into an Inner Coach. In turn, they will help your Tender Vulnerable Part (TVP) understand what it wants and needs, how to ask for it and receive it, and feel safe and supported again.

This is the end of Module 1, and what is intended to be the first week of the course. Take a few days to absorb this material.

Module 1 Review – Introduction to the Tools

Activity:

Watch Drama Triangle PowerPoint: https://www.slideshare.net/marva78/the-drama-triangle

Module 1 Quiz 2:

1) Which of the following are paired correctly?
   A. TVP – Creator
   B. Rescuer – Coach
   C. Persecutor – Challenger
   D. Victim – TVP
   E. All of the above
   F. A & C

2) What is the difference between the Rescuer and the Persecutor?
   A. Rescuer is positive and Persecutor is negative.
   B. Rescuer takes responsibility for things you have no control over, while Persecutor blames and criticizes.
   C. Rescuer helps you feel like you have control; Persecutor gives you ways to discharge the stored up energy of repressed emotions.
   D. Persecutor allies with TVP; Rescuer doesn't.
   E. B & C

3) (True or False) The following are all signs that you may be having an Emotional Flashback:
   ✓ You are caught in a loop of nonproductive thinking.
   ✓ Your thoughts are cycling between criticism, judgment and self-doubt.
   ✓ You are having trouble making important connections between cause and effect.
   ✓ You feel trapped in a sense of powerlessness or overwhelm.
   ✓ You feel as if you were helpless and dependent on others for your needs.

4) The following is true about Emotional Flashbacks:
   A. The feelings one has during an emotional flashback are extremely damaging and should be avoided at any cost.
   B. It is best to use punishment and ridicule to discourage people from taking refuge in an Emotional Flashback.
   C. There is nothing you can do to avoid making an Emotional Flashback worse.
   D. An Emotional Flashback is what happens when a person is triggered by an event that reminds them, at a subconscious level, of something stressful that happened in early childhood.

5) The following is true about Complex Post Traumatic Stress Disorder
   A. It is a disorder involving the failure to recover after a stressful event.
   B. It involves having frequent and/or prolonged emotional flashbacks.
   C. It affects a large percentage of care providers and helpers.
   D. It can actually help a person gain information vital to healing from early relational trauma.
   E. All of the above.

Module 2 - The Characters of Transformative Change

Tender Vulnerable Part (TVP) transforms into Creator

When using the Drama Triangle game as a starting point, I've found that the old name "Victim" brings up so much for people. So I decided to change the name to "Tender Vulnerable Part," because we all have one of these inside us. But how we react to our TVP is shaped largely by how we were received during our first three years by our caretakers. If our needs were met well, and our caretakers had some skill and were fairly consistent in responding to our dependence on them and our vulnerability, we learn to use this voice as our intuition. It helps us know what we like and by comparison what we don't like. And it can help us know when it's safe to relax and how to play.

If our needs were not met well, and our caretakers struggled with anxiety, depression or addiction, they likely became triggered when we reached out for help, when we became overwhelmed, or when we were making "too much" noise. They may have responded to us in our moments of greatest vulnerability by shaming us, shutting us down, or otherwise punishing us. People who experienced this kind of parenting in their first three years typically learn to abuse themselves in similar ways.

Between adults, whining or complaining is synonymous with "victimstance." It's failing to take adult responsibility to make necessary changes in one's life. But for a child, complaining is natural and adaptive. It's the only way to express what they need. It is literally:

☆ Crying out in displeasure.
☆ Crying out as an automatic physiological reaction to stress.
☆ Reaching for relief. – marijuana/adkana, food.

Children are designed to do this as a way to ensure their survival. When parents recognize the complaining for what it is, and tend to their children's normal human needs without reactivity or shame, the children are more likely to grow up able to form strong bonds, to trust themselves and others, and to have a reasonable ability to manage their own emotions. Unfortunately, when parents are traumatized themselves, or are under a lot of stress and lack support, they can respond to the child's needs in damaging ways. Their responses can teach the children to disconnect from their emotions, and that the only way they can be acceptable to their parents is if they hide their "undesirable" needs and feelings. As adults, when we hear this complaining or powerless voice coming from inside, we need to learn to pause, listen to ourselves with compassion, identify the things that we need, and then reach for them. Then, living life on life's terms from a state of peace and internal tranquility becomes more the norm than something only enjoyed by others.

The following table illustrates how the voice of the TVP can be connected to experiences from the first three years of life. In the left column, I offer examples of "TVP-talk." Rather than labeling it as "playing the Victim," I prefer to hear it with gentler ears, as we would hear a suffering child or infant. Notice the emotional response you have when you read over the list. When you notice "victimstance" inside your own head, do you automatically respond with a whole truckload of "shoulds," automatic shut-down, shame, or even despair? The right column contains phrases to watch for that represent how your inner relationships can show up in the outer world to help you become conscious of what's going on inside (also known as projection).

Tender Vulnerable Part (TVP)

TVP-Talk	Projections *(things to watch for)*
I'm uncomfortable and I can't do anything about it.	He/She kicks me when I'm down.
I have no choice in what happens to me.	
He/She has so much power/I have none.	She's compassionate with others, but not me. WTH?
He/She should be here for me.	
His/Her thoughts and opinions are stronger/more important than mine.	The way she is treating me is shocking.
My boss/partner is frightened and vulnerable (Therefore, I'm in BIG trouble)	
I've been thrown away.	What she does to me is overwhelming (short-circuit).
I am not valued (TERROR – I will suffer and die).	
People should not act this way.	
I am not experiencing love (when/where I should).	Other people are not valuing my position, experience, opinion.
This is not what I came here for (powerlessness).	
My voice isn't heard (frustration).	
There's no use complaining.	
I have no boundaries except the ones you give me.	Other people are not listening to me in general.
I don't know what to do/where to start.	
I'm lost.	
I don't have any options.	She doesn't love me.
I try, but nothing is working.	
I'm miserable.	Other people ignore what I say, don't recognize my value, contribution.
My choices are nothing without her support.	
Something is not right here (but I can't describe it with words).	

Where is the warmth/compassion I so desperately need?
In this moment (which is my entire reality) depending on others is:
    1) pointless, and
    2) making things even worse.
Betrayal
☆ She could help me, but she's not.
☆ I can't help myself.
My body is not cooperating.
☆ I don't have the <u>control that I need.</u>
I am in pain.
I can't do what I want.
She isn't attuning to my needs.
He/She is helping with things I don't need help with.
He/She is not helping me with my real needs.
Hurting me with her "help."
☆ She isn't there, and I need her.
She should be here to help me.
☆ I am totally helpless and dependent on her.
☆ I don't think I can handle this, the emotions are too much.
Rage
☆ Overwhelm
I can't regain my composure before the next wave of emotions/bad feelings hits.
I'm on my own.
☆ How could anybody possibly understand what I'm going through?
What did I do to cause this?
☆ Confusion (not able to connect logical cause and effect).
	The people I'm supposed to count on drain me.
	
	She is always finding fault with me.
	
	She is always picking on me.
	
	People criticize me unfairly.
	
	Other people like to tease me or make jokes about me.

Rescuer transforms into Coach

In a Drama Triangle game-playing family, it is relatively easy to catch ourselves using the Rescuer energy by asking: "Is this really any of my business?" In other words, "Am I doing for someone else something that they can or should actually be doing for themselves?" Similarly we can ask these questions of others in the family and see how they are assuming the Rescuer role.

With the Inner Drama Triangle, however, we are talking about how we developed internal "rescuing" strategies to cope with stress very early in life when we did not have what we needed, and we were not able to otherwise escape the stress or help ourselves. Our internal Rescuer energy takes the focus away from the pain and projects it outward. It involves taking responsibility for things we have no control over in attempts to feel that we have some control when we don't. The downside of Rescuer energy, however, is that in protecting TVP from painful feelings, it keeps TVP dependent in an unhealthy way. It does not promote growth or healthy individuation.

The strategies that infants and small children often use when their home does not feel safe to them and emotional needs for attunement are not being adequately met can include:

- ✓ "Getting small," or trying to be invisible in attempts to not be noticed.
- ✓ Disconnecting from overwhelming feelings.
- ✓ Taking responsibility for things we have no control over ("It must be my fault because I'm a bad kid," etc.).
- ✓ Extending attention outward and tending to others' needs.
- ✓ Adopting sterile choices (denial, cynicism, paranoia and self-betrayal, which mask rage, terror, and other uncomfortable feelings), in order to feel that we have at least some control over our lives.

When we learn to resort to Rescuer energy (what was once the best available "answer" to the problem of stress and discomfort), our brains adapt by forming automatic, well-worn grooves that favor those oft-repeated thoughts and behaviors. This has been described as "neurons that fire together wire together." Yes, it is real, but brains are also neuroplastic, which means that they are capable of growing and repairing for our entire lives.

Making the connections between what went on then and what's going on now is one of the ways we can re-wire the brain. Using focused attention helps us to form new neural pathways that allow us to see options that we hadn't noticed before, which help us feel more empowered. Some examples of using focused attention can include journaling, art or other physical, creative and/or expressive activities. At the end of this module, I will include a list of activities that can be used to focus your attention.

Journaling as a Way to Focus Attention

If you choose to journal, for example, you can write out the "story," using the dramatized, adrenaline-charged emotions that overcome you when you're in an emotional flashback, while holding the two stories (present and from childhood) together, and then notice how the energies match up. How old were you? What was going on for you? What was happening in your family? It was no doubt excruciating, though you have suppressed the intense emotions. It was unspeakably unpleasant, it was impossible to just relax and enjoy and safely explore your world. There is a tremendous loss to be grieved here. The loss of carefree childhood, play, abandon, freedom, and the opportunity to grow, connected naturally and reliably as part of a healthy family and community. Besides journaling, any other creative project will help to repair the brain and restore health, as long as you engage focused attention while simultaneously resisting the urge to resort to the old automatic internal patterns (represented by Persecutor and Rescuer).

When we notice Rescuer energy in our inner environment (examples of this in the table below), we can ask our Inner Rescuer to make a small pivot to the Coach character. In this way, we can move away from the knee-jerk reactions our brains have been wired to make (as a result of prolonged stress) to solutions that are more empowering and effective in the adult world. Remember that one of the things that makes the Drama Triangle so toxic is the unhealthy bond between TVP and Rescuer based on shame. When we resort to our old, tried-and-true defenses, we get the same result, over and over again. TVP agrees to remain dependent/powerless as an adult in order to "honor" Rescuer.

Rescuer

Rescuer-Talk	Projections (things to watch for)
I must have done something wrong (trying to figure out what it is). Maybe I can:	She blames me for everything.
Listen more carefully	
Smile bigger	
Not cry so much	
Be more grateful	
Not have so many needs	
Do something (anything) different	
Stop putting up with it	
Throw a tantrum	
Shut down	

It's my fault (I'm suffering because of my bad choices) obviously.	
I've allowed myself to be manipulated, so I must deserve this.	
I must be worthless.	
There is something wrong with me (I'm flawed somehow).	Other person belittling me
I'm shameful.	
No one can know me (because I'm too shameful).	
MASKING negative feelings to avoid being abandoned	After all I've done for him/her…(feeling bad when our kindness isn't reciprocated).
I have to hide from the world or bad things will happen.	Rescuing others, hoping they will return the favor.
I must hide my real self in order to be safe.	
Act in a way that makes everyone think I'm perfect.	She's punishing me (This is retaliation).
Put attention to suffering outside of self.	She wants me to suffer.
Caring for others at my expense. On borrowed: <ul><li>Time</li><li>Money</li><li>Energy</li></ul>	She is cruel. When I suffer, she is content, satisfied. She should not be happy when I am in pain or uncomfortable.
I'm punishing myself so maybe I can fix this.	Rejecting help because it's not real.
I should be punished. I want to be punished.	Gaslighting
Anticipate bad things so I can be prepared.	
Shut off caring.	
Shut down pain.	
Disconnect from feelings.	
It's better not to trust.	
Don't trust anyone/Don't depend on anyone but yourself.	
Don't dare trust that you can get help.	

Suspicion toward anything that claims to be "positive" "solution" "real support from another." I don't need help from her (Accept it: There is no help for me). Sterile choices of denial, cynicism, paranoia and self-betrayal. Going "crazy."	

When Rescuer shifts into the feminine energy of Coach, she can reclaim the power of Presence, attunement and awareness of emotions. Coach doesn't require TVP to remain powerless and dependent on her, but rather offers necessary attunement, nurture and support so that TVP can become empowered and move towards the Creator role.

Coach asks questions like: <div align="center">What do you need to feel a wee bit better? (Baby steps are just fine with Coach.) What are your heart's true desires? How can I help you figure that out?</div>

Her energy and her generous attention let you know that your emotions are not too much for her. *Let me cradle you until you feel better*, she might say. *Take the time you need. How are you feeling right now? How frustrated? How lonely? How scared? How overwhelmed? How tired? How discouraged? I'm right here with you; I'm not going anywhere, and I don't have anything else more important to do. It's safe to feel and notice the nuance of these feelings. I'm here to help you through this. You don't need to control or suppress it anymore. Surrender to it so that it can flow through you and resolve.*

This is the feminine energy of Coach. The energy of allowing, of relief, and ultimately of desire, of sweetness, of pleasure. Coach is also about receiving without resistance or judgment, and of gratitude. We will be talking about the masculine energy of Challenger next, but in our world of doing, accomplishment and taking charge, there is no shortage of in-charge/in-control masculine energy. Balance is what we are learning about here, and the power of feminine Presence, self-compassion and allowing energy!

Persecutor transforms into Challenger

Now let's meet the most obviously abusive part of the Drama Triangle, Persecutor. Persecutor tends to talk in a very compelling, powerful voice, and sometimes its message is so cloaked or only implied so that it's hard to recognize that it is abusive. Whatever the message, Persecutor energy feels condescending, blaming, shaming, criticizing. And knowing that it exists, and a little about how it works, can help you identify it.

One of the functions of Persecutor is to discharge the energy of unconscious anger, fear, powerlessness and frustration. The need to discharge this energy is real. But it can be done in healthy ways. When we notice Persecutor energy, it is our cue to take a step back and regroup. We can then ask Persecutor to shift and take the role of Challenger, who creates the safety and structure needed to make clear the logical steps necessary to reach our goals. Thus, the intense energy of Persecutor can shift to the powerful but non-violent masculine energy of Challenger, whose job it is to hold us accountable, but to do so wisely, with the focus on supporting our growth and learning.

Projection

For people who find themselves stuck in an emotional flashback, what's playing out in the world around them mirrors what's going on inside their minds. (The same is also true for people who are in perfect peace, and completely in their power. But that is a subject for another book.) This is confusing, but it also can be helpful because when it's projected onto someone else we can better see it, name it, and deal with it. With the right kind of help, it's easier to figure out what is going on, sort it out, and turn it around when other people are playing these parts for us. In the table below, the first column is the voice of Persecutor. The second column is how Persecutor Energy is projected out into the environment.

Notice how the column on the left could actually be the same as the one on the right. People who are triggered say the most outlandish, damaging things, so all of the things in the "Persecutor-Talk" column are also quite often heard in moments of tension, when people lash out, or speak before properly connecting with their deepest values or their self-respect.

Persecutor

Persecutor-Talk	Projections (things to watch for)
Shaming	Judging, Blaming, Criticizing, Comparing Contempt, Ridicule
Talking down (I have more experience, knowledge, I'm wiser, etc.)	"You always…"
Judging, Blaming, Criticizing, Ridiculing, Comparing	"You never…"
Here's what's wrong with you…	"You obviously…"
You always…	"What's wrong with you?"
You never…	"I'll tell you what you need…"
You obviously…	You're a piece of shit.
What's wrong with you?	"Here, let me do that for you, you obviously weren't paying attention when they were giving instructions."
Judging, Blaming, Criticizing, Ridiculing, Comparing	She's telling me how things are (like I'm stupid or something).
All the triggered adult caretaker's responses to a young child's vulnerability or complaining: <ul><li>You're over-reacting.</li><li>You're just trying to get attention.</li><li>You're just spoiled.</li></ul>	
I'll tell you what your problem is: <ul><li>There's something wrong with you.</li><li>Your needs are too much.</li></ul>	
I'll tell you what you need.	
You think you have it bad? This is nothing.	
I will totally give you something to cry about.	
You're doing this all wrong (you can't trust yourself).	
You should….	
You have to…	
You're in denial.	
Any form of punishment	

Contempt, judging, criticizing and blaming characterize Persecutor. This stance is just another defensive strategy that can become automatic when we witness contempt, judging, criticizing and blaming in our environment as children. We learn by watching our parents as they avoid their more tender feelings of fear, vulnerability, and sadness. Like Rescuer energy, Persecutor energy once offered us a viable solution to the problem of stress and discomfort, and our brains adapted by habituating those particular thoughts and behaviors.

When we notice contempt, judging, criticizing and blaming in our internal environment, we can begin to recognize them as red flags, indicating the need to pause, regroup, and shift to Challenger. Persecutor energy can be redirected so that it is actually very helpful, supplying essential masculine guidance, leadership and structure, helping TVP take steps toward re-establishing safety, relieving pain and replacing abuse with clarity. Challenger helps us to see how we have actually learned and gained wisdom from our experiences, however intense or impoverished, to become the resourceful individuals we are today.

It is important that we understand that these things we are hearing from Rescuer and Persecutor are merely relics from another time, or at the most, an oversimplified assessment of reality. They developed to protect us from becoming overwhelmed with feelings of vulnerability, sadness, neediness, or fear at a time when we were not yet developed enough to handle these emotions without the support and attention of a safe adult other.

Questions Challenger might ask in order to hold us accountable:

What is your intention here?
In your most empowered moments, what have you learned that your parents didn't teach you and your younger self never knew?
What would it take to own and embody this information – to really make it yours?
In what ways has this ego defense actually served you?
What need does this automatic behavior fulfill?
In what ways does it need to be honored?
What is it telling you?
How can it be used for good?
How can the energy of the previously unwanted emotions be discharged consciously and safely?

Focused Attention Activities

Focused attention actually re-wires the brain (when you can successfully resist a compulsion or an urge). This activity through which you choose to focus your attention can be anything meaningful and/or productive that requires your attention. The idea is to do something that feels somewhat better than ruminating, and helps distract you from the looping or repeating pattern that has been going on in your mind/system.

Where attention goes, neural firing flows, and neural connection grows.

- Daniel J Siegel, MD

Choose an activity that appeals to you, and practice it for 10-20 minutes.

I include a few suggestions on the following pages. They fall into several categories. The possibilities are endless, but the activity needs to work for you!

Physical/Energetic (pg 32)

Movement and Music (pg 36)

Interpersonal (pg 37)

Mental (pg 39)

Imaginal (pg 64)

Physical/Energetic Focused Attention Activities

1) TET Holding Position (pg 33)
2) Walking Meditation (pg 35)

Other Ideas:

Ohm Alone or With Others
Chant Alone or With Others
Focus attention on the breath. Extended phrases, extended exhalation.

TET: Trauma Elimination Technique
Developed by Janae B. Weinhold, Ph.D. LPC

Janae's many years of work in clearing trauma in herself and with her clients validated that it was possible to truly clear trauma from your nervous system, brain and behavioral responses. She says that the **Trauma Elimination Technique (TET)** is not only the most effective tool she's ever used, but that it allows you to really take charge of your own healing process. She also likes it because you can use it yourself when you really need it. This empowering aspect is really important for people who have been traumatized and for whom disempowerment and helplessness have become so familiar.

TET is a synthesis of a number of trauma healing modalities including the Tapas Acupressure Technique (TAT), EMDR (Eye Movement Desensitization and Reprocessing) and Thought Field Therapy (TFT). In the extensive use of TET on herself and her clients, she discovered that it not only cleared trauma from present-life experiences, but also from other dimensions of realities, such as past lives.

If you wish TET to clear traumas held in other realities, just set this intention before you begin to use it. If this idea intimidates you, set your intention to only clear present-life trauma. You are always in charge when using TET. Here is the procedure.

Step 1: Learn the TAT holding pose.
  a) Use one hand to hold three points on your face. Touch the points lightly:
   1. Touch thumb just above or adjacent to the inner corner of one eye.
   2. Place the end of your ring (4th) finger just above and adjacent to the inner corner of the other eye.
   3. Place the end of your middle finger on an indentation in the middle of your forehead about ½" higher than your eyebrows.
  b) Place your other hand palm down at the back of your head just below the bump at the bottom of your skull (the occipital ridge), centering it at the midline.
  c) Once you have learned this pose, go directly to Step 2.

Step 2: Identify the trauma you want to work on. This should be one particular trauma, not one that is long-term or recurring.
  a) Focus your attention on a picture about this trauma.
  b) Notice what thoughts go with this picture.
  c) Identify the belief about yourself that goes with this picture.
  d) Notice what emotion you feel when you see this picture, think these thoughts, and believe this belief.

Step 3: Simultaneously hold the picture, thoughts, belief and the feelings while doing the TAT holding pose. Remain in this pose until you feel something happen internally (different for each person: a subtle shift of energy, a feeling of relaxation, a deep sigh – or for one minute, whichever comes first).

Step 4: Notice where you have been holding tension in your body related to the picture/thoughts/belief/feelings and focus your attention in this place while continuing to hold the TAT pose. Remain in this pose until you feel the shift or for one minute.

Step 5: Zero in on a "hot spot."
   a) Focus on the picture/thought/belief/feeling.
   b) Do the TAT holding technique until you feel a shift.
   c) Focus on the "storage place" in your body where you hold tension related to this memory while using the TAT holding technique until you feel a shift.

Step 6: Continue returning to the original picture and reviewing it until there are no more hot spots.

Step 7: Drink a glass of water immediately after completing a session. Be sure to drink another eight glasses in the next 24 hours to help the toxins released by the TET procedure leave your body.

Walk for 10-20 minutes, keeping your attention on your body.

- How do your feet hit the ground (heel first, ball first?)
- Are your toes crunched or spread?
- How do your calves feel?
- What happens when you push off from the ball of the foot?
- Is your chest open?
- Are your shoulders back and down?
- Is your chin jutting out ahead of you?
- Where is your center of gravity?
- Do your arms swing in the opposite direction as your feet?
- Imagine holding a light, porcelain urn on top of your head. It is fragile and precious.
- Allow your hips to be the shock absorbers, compensating for the movement of the feet and legs so that the top half of your body can glide along unaffected.
- Push off from the ball of your foot with each step and notice what happens in your hips and calves.

Movement & Music
Focused Attention Activities

Trance Dance

http://www.tonirahman.com/wp-content/uploads/2017/04/Trance-Dance-as-Focused-Attention.pdf

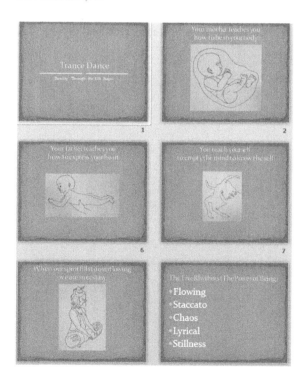

Other suggestion:

Listen to any music with a positive message

Interpersonal Focused Attention Activities

Talking and Listening
Attending a 12-Step Meeting

| Al-Anon/ Alateen | Alcoholics Anonymous | Narcotics Anonymous | Cocaine Anonymous | Sex and Love Addicts Anonymous | Overeaters Anonymous | Nar-Anon | Co-Dependents Anonymous |

Who Are Al-Anon Members?

Al-Anon members are people, just like you, who are worried about someone with a drinking problem.

Mental
Focused Attention Activities

Visioning (pg 40)
Manifesting (pg 42)
Four-Step Approach to Responding to Urges and Compulsions (pg 44)
Mother Exercise (pg 46)
Father Exercise (pg 48)
Mourning in Giraffe (pg 50)
Significant Traumas and Betrayals (pg 52)
Transforming Shoulds (pg 54)
Capturing the Voices of Your Internal Parts (pg 56)
Rite of Passage – Adolescence Exercise (pg 58)
Write a letter to yourself from your Inner Feminine (pg 60)
Write a letter to yourself from your Inner Masculine (pg 62)

Other suggestions:

Reading a book you like
Journaling

Visioning

This is a practice that I have been using for many years. It was inspired by Shakti Gawain in her book, *Creative Visualization*, but it has evolved as I've used it over the years. Start with the list of categories below to describe the things and conditions you desire in your life. Modify it so that it suits you and your life. Don't hesitate to write down what you already like about the way things are going in each category. But allow yourself to take sweeping liberties, embellish, and stretch your imagination, reaching for what you would really like – what would make your life even better. Keep a copy of your visioning statement in a place where you can find it later and update it as you accomplish what you set out to do and notice changes in what you are desiring. You can also make a list of 10 things that you want (but don't know how you could ever afford). Be extravagant, and see what happens. It's okay to want more!

I surrender to my soul's deepest intent
for this lifetime.
I Am Joy-Filled and Grateful!

These are the details of my desired life:

Work
Professional Growth
Finances
Relationships
Healthy Adult Intimacy
Creative Life
Co-workers
Growth
Body
Recreation
Home
Rhythms
Community
Spiritual

I thank you Spirit; I thank you Angels, and so it is!

This or something better now manifests
for the highest good of all concerned.

Manifesting

Materials:
- Old magazines
- Scissors
- Small box
- Paper
- Pen

Procedure: Find some old magazines and flip through the pages. Notice textures and colors and let your eyes linger on the ones that feel pleasing to you. Find pictures that you would like to look at some more, or that represent things you want. Cut out the pictures that you like and collect them in the box.

On the outside of the box, write, *"Whatever is contained in this box IS."*

For each picture that you collected in the box, write on a slip of paper what it represents that you would like more of in your life. What you are writing on each slip of paper is a thing, a condition, or an experience you want to have in your life. Be as specific as you can when you write what you want. The more details the better. Continue to add slips of paper as you think of things, conditions or experiences that you want to have.

Read through the slips of paper and look at the pictures you have collected two or three times a week and let yourself anticipate what it will feel like when these things are a real part of your life. Thank your box and your inner Creator for helping you to get clearer about what you want more of in your life.

Four-Step Approach to Responding to Urges and Compulsions

1) Name the experience (just naming it helps reduce the stress).
- I am aware that I'm having a compulsion to ___check social media___.
- I'm aware that I'm having this sensation of ___emptiness___.
- I'm aware that I'm having the emotion of ___loneliness /___ because of *I'm not doing anything*

boredom / laziness

2) Frame the behavior and identify its function in the past.
- This makes sense because this is what my brain learned to do when I felt powerless, etc.

or
- It's just my younger scared self; she has a real need, and I am interested in identifying and tending to it.

or
- This is happening because I need:
  o a sense of relief.
  o a way to escape.
  o a way to express my voice.
  o etc.

• a way to see what those around me are doing
• a way to imagine another person's life → turn to fiction
↳ imagine my life → collage

3) Ask: How would I like this to go differently?

Example: *I see myself being able to excuse myself briefly (to check in with myself) instead of pretending that I'm engaged in a conversation (but I'm really shutting down and waiting for it to be over).*

4) Concentrate on something other than the urge (Focused Attention).

(REPEAT AS NECESSARY)

Focused attention actually re-wires the brain (when you can successfully resist the urge). This activity through which you focus your attention can be anything meaningful and productive that requires your attention.

Modified from Alsana Treatment Center for Eating Disorders
See also www.Urge911.com

- Compulsion to check email, check my phone, check meetup
- sensation of boredom
- emotion of uneasiness b/c I want to see what's new
- brain learned to do it to get stimuli,
- need for dopamine (accomplishment)
- I would like more focus, less hive mind, less of "let me share this m" & more of structured time
  ↳ resist the urge.

Mother Work

Three things I love about my mother:

Three things I hate about her:

Three wishes for her:

Three resentments I have toward her:

When comparing myself with my mother, I can see how we have the following in common:

Father Work

We all have a father. Whether his role in your life was to provide the DNA for your genetic makeup or to raise and mentor you; to play with you and teach you about the world, he provides an indelible impression that impacts you and how you relate to men and the world. And whether he is known to you or not, living or not, you can still benefit from exploring your relationship with him.

Writing Exercise

1. Using a separate journal or several sheets of paper, write down any memories you have about your father from your early years. Even if they are just glimpses, or impressions.
2. What have you heard from relatives and other community members about your father? What was he like from their perspective? Does that match up with your observations and experience of him?
3. How did your father step up for you? What moved him? What were his dreams and aspirations, his values?
4. Bring an image of his face or his physical essence into your imagination and notice how your body feels.
5. Imagine the smallness of yourself when you were 4 or 5 years old, and think about his physical largeness in comparison to you. Imagine your five-year-old self in a room you would have likely inhabited with your father. How does that feel? Do you make contact? What kind? Are you touching, talking, laughing, cowering, uncomfortable, insecure?
6. If your father was active in your life, he was likely one of the people who introduced you to the world in one way or another. Write about how he acted as a bridge to the larger world, outside of the home.
7. What would you most like your father to know about you, from the perspective of your 10 year old self? Write for 10 minutes whatever comes to mind. If nothing comes to mind, how do you feel about that?
8. Visit your teenage self and bring to mind a time you were in the presence of your father. Notice the physical proximity. Notice if this feels different from before.
9. Based on how he interacted with you (or didn't), what do you think your father thought of you? In what ways did he approve of you, your behaviors, your appearance, your clothing, your mannerisms, your accomplishments, your personality?
10. What did your father do that annoyed you most?
11. What did he not do that impacted you the most?
12. What happened to your father that accounts for his deficits?
13. Were/Are you afraid of your father? Why?
14. Were/Are you worried about him? Why?

15. Were/Are you angry with him? Why?

16. What good things did you get from your father directly or indirectly?

17. What did he believe about the world? How does that compare with what you believe about the world?

18. If your father is no longer living, how has this changed how you feel about him?

19. If you could change one thing about your father, what would it be?

20. Think about the men in your life who have contributed positively, who have supported you in some way, even if from a distance. Make a list of those gifts and qualities, and feel your gratitude toward them.

21. One by one, write out a complete list of characteristics, or things that endear these people to you, or inspire you.

22. Notice how these characteristics exist, also, in you, or you are – right now – in the process of developing them.

23. Imagine an "other-worldly" father that is a conglomerate of all the positive attributes that you have experienced in the men you have known (or experienced from a distance), and let yourself enjoy how that feels. If you can conjure an image, let yourself do that to add another layer of validity to this entity so you can more easily retrieve him in the future.

24. Find a name that fits this "other-worldly father" that you like, and that feels just right. Notice where and how you feel that in your body.

25. Know that this feeling is available to you anytime you direct your energy here. It belongs to you, and nobody can take it away from you.

Mourning in Giraffe

This is a process to heal ourselves concerning a choice we made in the past that we now regret. It is a way of acknowledging our regret and of empathizing with ourselves so we can grow beyond our past limitations.

Perhaps we may think we are "correcting the situation" or "making up" for a past mistake by continuing to blame ourselves and prolonging our sense of guilt and shame. Yet, as St. Frances de Sales wrote, "Those who are fretted by their own failings will not correct them. All profitable corrections come from a calm and peaceful mind."

There is a belief in our culture that the suffering of the perpetrator makes up for the loss that victims undergo – an eye for an eye. As a practitioner of NVC, if I lose an eye as a consequence of your behavior, I know my deep need for empathy, compassion, safety, etc., will not be met by your offering me either your self-judgment or your eye. I will be able to receive what I need from you only after you have taken the much harder path of truly mourning the choices you have made. The healing between us will happen when I can hear the depth of your mourning and you can offer me the depth of empathy that I need.

Use the following to mourn a choice you made in the past that you now regret.

a. Observation: what I said or did in the past that I now regret:

b. Self-judgments: what I think of myself for having done or said (a)

c. Current feelings and needs: translate self-judgments into feelings and needs

d. Empathy for myself: determine what need I was trying to fulfill when I chose to take the action or say the words I now regret

e. Current request of myself:

Aware of my current feelings and unfulfilled needs (c), I would like to address my needs (d) in the following manner:

This exercise comes from *Nonviolent Communication Companion Workbook*, by Lucy Leu, pg 124-25.

Significant Traumas and Betrayals

Make a list of all the significant betrayals you have experienced in your life, whether you were the person betrayed or the person who betrayed someone else. After making your list, journal on the questions below.

- What similarities are there between these traumas?

- What were the circumstances?

- How did I feel in each betrayal or trauma?

- What beliefs, values, assumptions and expectations have I formed about myself and about the world as a result of all these traumas and betrayals?

- How does my earliest trauma replay over and over in my life?

- What dramas seem to play over and over?

- What was unfinished about each of the trauma/betrayal experiences?

- What do I need to do to finish each of these experiences?

- Look at your life drama to see what isn't finished. Examine each event or betrayal to see what you need to do to complete it.

Barry & Janae Weinhold, Colorado Institute for Conflict Resolution and Creative Leadership

Transforming Shoulds

Shoulds signal that we are afraid. They are a collection of hard-to-verbalize feelings, but if we can get them down in writing, we can begin to transform them into feelings and needs. What follows is how it looks to transform shoulds into feelings and needs.

Outer Shoulds	Taking responsibility for our feelings and needs looks like this:
• People shouldn't make "incorrect" assumptions.	When people make assumptions, I feel angry, because I need respect.
• People should get my permission before entering my house or touching my things.	When people enter my house without permission I feel startled, alarmed and defensive because I need safety and dependability.
• People shouldn't touch or take my things without my permission or some kind of prior understanding.	When people touch or take my things I feel violated and defensive. I need gentleness, respect, and consideration.

See if you can capture the shoulds that have been lurking in your mind. If you can catch them, they will help you identify feelings and needs.

Inner Shoulds	Taking responsibility for feelings and needs:

Inner Shoulds	Taking responsibility for feelings and needs:

Capturing the Voices of Your Internal Parts

The ego is a head trip, groups of words that form themselves into repetitive patterns that chatter continuously like crickets in our mind.

-Gabrielle Roth

We all contain multitudes. Great thinkers like Freud, Carl Jung, Walt Whitman, Alfred Adler, Richard Schwartz, have long recognized this.

In this exercise, pay close attention to the various aspects of your inner self. Notice how they are in conflict, allied or at odds with each other. How they protect, rescue or war with each other. With each one in turn, tune in so that you can better hear their frequency, as if they are their own radio station. Invite them to speak clearly so that you really know them. Their needs, their fears, their experience of the world.

Feel into their essence. When did they first appear, and for what reason?

Can you see them? Could you draw or paint them? Write about how they appear, any physical attributes, how old they seem. What their favorite expressions are, their general attitudes. Get curious about what they are doing. How does each of them serve you? What greater purpose do they serve? What do they like and dislike?

See if you can capture the voice and tone of your internal parts in the space below, and then continue in your journal if you like. Write without censoring or editing your work for 10-20 minutes.

That I am mean, not easy to talk to   vs   I have no boundaries. When I state a boundary, i comes off as selfish & not caring

I stayed in the triangle for too long, chasing for the role of persecutor & victim, saying things like "they say things about you too" ready to damage her with phrases like she'll never be rich which is an exaggeration. Things like that are cruel. She said no one wants to speak to me. Is there a projection? I think it's about saying mean things to people. I've talked shit & it's something I look down at now.

The conflict is that I can swing – they said I'm mean/selfish, I don't want to do this ~~with their~~ now. They say mean things, they don't respond in a way that is thoughtful. I can continue to interact with them or I can distance my self – they can try to manipulate you by saying you're selfish for letting me support you & now you're doing x, y, z. This is enmeshment

Are you doing it to ~~support~~ assist me, or are you doing it so I can support you?
in getting where I want to be.

I'm allowed to state what I do & do not want to do, especially b/c

| I value | love strength resilience effort gratitude | I want to step out of the trial if some |

I have a need for love – hearing ppl say that I'm selfish, can't be talked to, mean – makes me feel disconnected & alone. I have a need to be understood, not expected to take a course to fill my sisters face and a lack of doing that means I'm mean

I have a need to state my abilities. I don't need to feel inadequate for not being able to do them

I don't need to feel ~~guilty~~ down for asking for what I want
        – for stating what I'm willing & not willing to do

Rite of Passage - Adolescence

The following exercise ideas are designed to help you revisit your adolescence in a new way. Adolescence is a time of profound change, not only in terms of responsibility and physical maturity, but also in terms of identity and societal expectations. The main developmental task of adolescence is individuating from parental influence - to begin to form a unique set of values that is not identical to what he or she has been taught. Use a journal or loose paper to write out your thoughts. Write until you have answered the questions, and then keep writing until you have fully expressed yourself. Chances are, your adolescent self was not listened to as much as he or she wanted or needed to be. You can change that now.

1. Think about your adolescence in relation to your mother. How did your relationship change? As you began to look more like an adult and less like a child, did she see this and feel excited and proud? Or did this seem to mark a time of less closeness, more conflict? What did your growing up mean to her?

2. Think about your adolescence in relation to your father. How did your relationship change? As you began to look more like an adult and less like a child, what happened to your relationship with your father? Did he acknowledge you as a person, or as an extension of himself? What did your growing up mean to him?

3. When did you first start noticing that your parents made mistakes, that they were just imperfect humans? Write about a few of the mistakes your parents made and notice any feelings that come up when you tell these stories. See if you can name the feelings, whether they are of the emotional variety, or if they are physical sensations in your body or your energy field.

4. Write about some of the worst mistakes you made as a teenager, and then about how your parents responded. This is not a time to see things from their perspective, but from yours. Describe what happened to the best of your ability. See if you can name your feelings fully and completely. Stand by your adolescent self while he or she pours this story out onto the page. Let yourself say what you couldn't have when you were a teenager. This time and space is just for you. It's about time you had a place just for this purpose.

5. What are the things you would not want to change about the way you were raised?

6. Write about any mentors or role models you had during your adolescent years. What roles did they play and how did they change the trajectory of your life?

7. Write briefly or in depth about your own sexual history. Document landmarks with regard to physical development and the people in your life at that time. Remember your first crush, your first boyfriend or girlfriend. Remember body sensations and write about them. What do you like to remember about this time? What would you rather forget? What do you remember about your body? Your tender unguarded self? Your mind?

8. Make a list of the feminine aspects of yourself – the sensitive, empathic, warm, receptive, intuitive side of you. Can you see her? Feel her essence? Does she have a name? Thank her for showing up.

9. Make a list of the masculine aspects of yourself – the active, analytical, outgoing, physical, get-things-done, practical side. Can you see him? Feel his essence? Does he have a name? Thank him for showing up.

10. Imagine how these two aspects of yourself might interact with one another. Explore how their roles work together to support your growth, your development, and the ease in which you can step gracefully and confidently into adulthood and your fullest potential.

From Your Inner Feminine (sample):

My Beloved One,

I adore you. You are a child of God. You have my full permission to be all you came here to be. Take your time. Take all the time you need. I am strong enough to support you, while you explore who you are and what you will do next and next and next. How precious you are to me. I can't wait to see what you next discover about yourself, your strengths, your yet unexplored gifts and qualities and potentials. I give you permission and my blessing to indulge in pleasure, to explore the world, inner and outer, to be great, to be vulnerable, to be playful, to be a beginner - to be exactly who you are now. I am holding this space and time for you while you do this very important work. Go ahead. Let yourself feel your emotions. It is safe to be in your body now. Listen to what it tells you. I will offer you guidance and direction through your sensory experience and I encourage you to enter the full expression of your deepest self, from this moment onward. You are enough. You are so precious to me. I love you so.

I will be here for you always.

Your Inner Feminine

Now write a letter from your Inner Feminine.

From Your Inner Masculine (sample letter*):

My Dearest Beloved,

It has been a great loss that I have not been more apparent to you during the first part of your life. I therefore step up and fully assume this position now. From the moment you were born it has been clear to me how unique and beautiful you are. Take these truths now into your heart and mind. They are true, and I have no reason to deceive you.

If it is your desire, I give you permission, now, to be all you came here to be, to be a woman in all senses of the word - to experience the joy of physical mastery and pleasure. Precious one, you are the master of your experience and it is yours to explore pleasure and find what gives you joy and fulfillment. Know that this sometimes is best done by experiencing what you don't like, but it does not always have to be so.

Go ahead. Take those steps. I will be here to support you if you're not sure at first. I am here. I will continue to be here, whatever direction you decide to go, you will not disappoint me. I promise you this. Trust yourself. Your instincts are good. Your judgment, your discernment can be trusted. I am so proud of you, and excited about this work you have been doing, and what you will do next.

I love you. You deserve deep satisfaction, contentment, and the fulfilment of your heart's desires. You are good. You are pure. You are kind. You are enough.

Go forth. Be yourself.

Your Inner Masculine.

*Adapt as necessary so that gender feels appropriate, remembering that we all have both feminine and masculine aspects.

Write a letter from your Inner Masculine

Imaginal
Focused Attention Activities
(practice for 10-15 minutes)

Imagine chopping wood.

Imagine running.

Imagine the most beautiful rose you have ever seen. Destroy it. Repeat.

Monitoring Your Inner Environment

What kind of "inner environment" do you wish to experience? It is common for children to disconnect from feelings and needs when their parents aren't positioned to help them with the monumental developmental task of learning to understand and regulate their emotions. In many homes, children are strongly discouraged from expressing or even having emotions. In such cases, children learn by example that suppressing or punishing are the appropriate responses to emotions. If you notice that you are punishing yourself as a way to make yourself "behave," it is a good time to notice that, and re-think your strategy. You do not deserve to be punished. Developing self-punishing behaviors in childhood is a normal and adaptive thing to do when one's parents are not able to help them deal with their emotions in healthier ways. Another way to look at this is that a child learns to do – in an environment in which emotions are wrong – whatever it takes to disconnect from their feelings.

So as you gradually learn that feelings are actually very important and functional AND that you can use them, express them and regulate them without hurting people, your need to disconnect will feel less and less urgent.

Module 2 Exercise: Over the course of the next week, pay special attention to what you think and say to yourself. Use the following page to jot down the actual words that come up in your head during the situation. Later in the day or week, review what you observed of your thoughts and inner dialogues. Were there judgments of yourself, the situation, or other people? Did your thoughts embody other forms of life-alienating communication (complaining, comparing, criticizing, looping thoughts of any kind)? Was there revulsion or general dislike of something you were doing or someone you came into contact with? If so, these might be early signs of "anger," signaling that you need to attend to boundary issues (which requires checking in to see what unmet needs you have at the moment, and then attending to them ASAP). We will talk more about "early" anger in Module 5.

Remind yourself each day to be alert for external and internal messages that contribute to disconnection from feelings and needs. Notice the times you hear or say (to yourself) any of the following words: should, must, can't, have to, supposed to, ought to. Be aware of moments when you use shaming, contempt or punishment as a strategy for staying disconnected from your more vulnerable emotions. For many of us, these things were so commonplace in our homes growing up, that they now seem normal to us. They are actually warning signs:

Should	Shaming (the self)
Must	Contempt (toward yourself)
Can't	Punishment (of the self)
Have to	Judgments (of anyone, including the self)
Supposed to	Comparing (self to others)
Ought to	

Be sure to re-visit what you have written later on, when you have some time. When you do, see if you can begin to translate these expressions into feelings and needs.

In Other Words...

Inner Masculine (Left Brain)	Inner Feminine (Right Brain)
The Inner Masculine is the part of the healthy psyche that represents surrender to the soul's clamoring potential; the willingness to take charge of life without guilt. Inner Masculine also supports safety and accountability by providing structure, encouraging learning and identifying next steps.	The Inner Feminine is the part of the healthy psyche that reconnects an individual with his or her fullest potential.
Questions Inner Masculine asks:	Inner Feminine is characterized by her compassion, comforting and nurturing. She provides attunement, encouragement and support. She helps an individual recognize where he or she has inadvertently given their power away, and helps them set that right. With personal power reestablished, she encourages true independence and healthy interdependence and with the help of Inner Masculine clears away resistance to receiving what delights her.
What is my intention in this situation? What has happened to me? Is there something I can do to further my learning and growth here? What would it take for me to be willing to take charge of my life without guilt or shame? In what ways has this (automatic response) actually served me? How can the energy of this emotion be discharged safely? What need does this emotion/ attitude/ belief fulfill? In what ways does it need to be honored? What is it telling me? How can I use it for good?	If we listen, she says to us, "I see this is difficult for you. Let me hold you until you feel better." She might ask us:
	What is crying out for attention here? What needs to be met with compassion and care? Are you frustrated? Are you lonely? How lonely? Are you scared? How scared? Are you overwhelmed? Are you tired? Are you discouraged? What would it take to move in the direction of relief?
	"I'm right here with you," she is likely to tell us. "Take your time. It's safe to feel and notice the nuance of these feelings. You have the support you need. Don't avoid or try to control your feelings. Surrender to them so that they can flow through you and resolve, leaving you changed and free."

This is the end of Module 2, and what is intended to be the second week of the course. Take a few days to absorb this material. Begin to monitor your inner environment, and make that a regular part of your daily routine. Join the private Facebook group, Self Abuse & The Inner Drama Triangle, if you have questions or would like to know what other students are sharing.

Ask to Join here: https://www.facebook.com/groups/1039378412862770/

Module 2 Review –The Characters of Transformative Change

Activities:

If you have not done so already, please join the private Facebook group here: https://www.facebook.com/groups/1039378412862770/

Begin to monitor your inner environment on a daily basis.

If you notice yourself engaging in negative self-talk or otherwise lapse into looping thoughts, compulsive behaviors or addictive behaviors, take 10 to 20 minutes and do a Focused Attention Activity.

Module 2 Quiz 1:

1) (True or False) Everyone has tender vulnerable parts inside even if they try to keep them hidden.

2) What is the critical time period in which parents need to be emotionally available to their children to ensure the ability of the child to later form healthy relationships and regulate their emotions?
   A. The first sixteen years
   B. The first three years
   C. The first six weeks
   D. The first five years

3) Having our needs met well as children involves:
   A. Being given everything we ask for.
   B. Being with our parents 100% of the time.
   C. Fairly predictable and compassionate responses from our parents when we are frightened or uncomfortable.
   D. Being seen and not heard.
   E. Looking good, and making sure the family looks good.

4) The following are commonly responsible when children's needs are not met well:
   A. Poverty
   B. Intergenerational Trauma
   C. Mental Illness
   D. Addiction
   E. All of the above

Module 3 - TVP Shifts to Creator

Drama Triangle Dynamics as Trauma

When children experience Drama Triangle dynamics in their home environment and it becomes their model for relating, they often miss out on opportunities to develop healthy relational skills and useful problem solving skills. This chaotic dynamic then becomes their inner blueprint for dealing with stress. In fact many researchers in the field of attachment today believe that the Drama Triangle is the primary cause of trauma and disease. The good news: Whether we witnessed healthy interactions between our parents or not, it is always possible to create a healthier inner environment.

It is essential that you understand that the parts of you that get upset, feel vulnerable, and have needs are all normal. Just like you needed to be listened to when you were small, they actually need to be listened to. They are not just whining, spoiled children. They are important pieces of yourself; they have valuable wisdom, and as you learn their language, you learn more about who you really are. Not having a steady source of compassionate attention (attunement) for whatever reason was extremely stressful for us as children, and made us resort to ego defenses in order cope.

Complaining

Complaining is actually a really great thing. If we are paying attention, it alerts us to a need for something that we're afraid to ask for. Once we realize we are complaining, we can pause, engage our curiosity and ask, *What is all this whining about? What have I been afraid to ask for?* Coach and the Inner Feminine can help us remember that we are powerful and that we must reach for what we desire.

TVP is that little child in all of us. It serves the important role of knowing what we like and don't like. She/He does this in whatever way she/he can. In the following sections, we will be learning how to turn TVP energy into Creator energy. Creator energy is clear, direct, simple and we want to encourage it. It knows what it knows and feels what it feels. Unencumbered by shoulds and shame, it delights in the sweetness of life.

Creator Energy looks like this:

This is what I want!
Yummy!
What's that?
Receptivity to growth and new information
Why?
Attraction to novelty.
I don't like that!
No!
Mine!

Intimately knowing what we desire is a little scary for people who have spent their lifetimes studying the preferences of others and being more sensitive to others' needs than their own. For those people, maybe it will take a little pressure off just to know that it could take some time and patience to figure out what you want, and that's normal. You can allow yourself as much time as you need, and take baby steps. It is even possible to be very clear on some of the things you desire without being clear on all the things you desire. The important thing is to spend more time and energy enjoying the process of self-exploration, noticing and paying attention to what we like and want more of, and less time feeling like an overwhelmed, powerless, voiceless child. We do have control over that. We are all Creators, and we can have what we desire.

Recognizing Complaining

If you notice you don't feel right, or kind of like there is a cloud hanging over your head, stop and check to see what is going on inside. If you notice that you are "complaining" inside or feeling powerless, hopeless, triggered, or overwhelmed, you can use that as a cue that you have fallen into an emotional flashback, and that you can learn to turn to your inner parents for empathy and support. When in an emotional flashback, you do not have access to your resources, or memory of ever feeling okay. A well-established set of inner parents can help you figure out what is needed in order to feel better. what do I need?

Sometimes hanging out in the TVP role of the Internal Drama Triangle is so familiar that you don't even realize you're doing it. That's why it's sometimes good to get feedback from someone you trust. They will tell you if you seem regressed or disconnected from your power. The following list will help you know what to look for to identify the complaining energy of your TVP.

Persistent Feelings of Powerlessness
Surges of Overwhelm

Undercurrents of Betrayal
Feeling like a shamed or powerless child
Comparing yourself with others

Play

The most important responsibility of children is to play, which, as it turns out, is crucial to healthy brain development. Play is spontaneous and pleasure driven. It involves flow – full immersion, energized focus. In play, we can be creative – with our defenses and need for control turned off, we can enter into rich creative realms by ourselves and in the company of others. Play is a learning medium for all of us. But it is simply not possible to lose ourselves in play if we do not feel safe.

Stuart Brown researches play. He says that we are designed to play our whole lifetime, and that, ironically, play deprivation is linked to violent crime. Research, then, is telling us that play is practical, necessary for learning and crafting the brain, and that it is the opposite of depression. Among the various benefits of play, he cites the following:

It increases innovation.
It increases feelings of belonging.
It allows us to explore the possible.
It overrides power differentials.
It is the "basis for human trust established through play signals."
It promotes the development of emotion regulation.
It fires up the cerebellum, the frontal lobe, and contextual memory.

What Blocks/Prevents Play?

- Lack of Safety
- Defense against an unsafe environment turns off all the mammalian innovations of the autonomic nervous system (ANS) – especially the face-heart connection. (When upper face is animated, vagal activity to the heart is calming.)
- Programming - Our society does not value play (except in certain, controlled venues).
- Fear
- Rigidity – need for predictability
- Anticipation of the future
- Need to be in control
- Perfectionism – "mistakes are dangerous"
- Resentment
- Bogged down in the past

Realize that there are many reasons why it has been difficult to relax enough to play, especially when play involves other people. The fact is, we need to have a secure base in order to feel courageous enough to venture out into the unpredictability of play. As you feel more and more masterful with your self-parenting abilities, you will be able to drop your defenses, experience the magic of spontaneity and the present moment, and lose yourself in play. Until then, know that play is an important part of a balanced, productive life.

It might also be necessary to examine the things that you have learned about play. When families are in crisis, they are often isolated, stressed, and everything is serious. It is often more important to be quiet and invisible than to enjoy and have fun. That's why it may take some time for you to really feel that it's okay to do things on a whim, that it's okay to make mistakes, and that it's even okay to appear flaky or even draw attention to yourself sometimes. The importance of creating an appearance of having it all together is paramount in dysfunctional homes. Therefore, it may take some work for you to give yourself permission to relax and sidestep the impulse to "be perfect."

The HUGE Feelings: Rage, Grief, Despair, Terror & Attraction

Coach is Divinely Equipped to Help Us with Our HUGE Feelings

This section is called HUGE Feelings for a reason. As small children, emotions are something that we can only develop through our interactions with others. And it can be truly terrifying to be dependent on another for our very lives, if there is only one designated "other" and that "other" is not adequately supported, connected, attentive and receptive to our needs.

There is so much old pain and discomfort behind these feelings. This is the pain of your TVP. At the time you first felt them, you were too young to talk. You had not developed enough cognitive capacity to understand or manage them. Your brain has done a great deal of developing since that time, and now, familiarity and habits are the only things keeping you from connecting with, experiencing and properly managing your feelings.

The energy of Coach can support a gentle shift from TVP to Creator. Coach's keen attunement allows her to feel into your needs and desires and help you find just the right words to express them. With Coach's gentle presence, Creator readily knows: What do I desire? As TVP pivots to Creator, the courage to yearn is reignited. When the feelings come up, gently receive them. With the support of Challenger and the presence and compassion of Coach, they are no longer frightening or overwhelming. They are TVP's purest expression. They are safe to explore and you are now reconnected with "yourself."

Listening to our HUGE Feelings with Compassion

Bring to mind a beloved child, an infant, or a helpless animal. Return to this beloved, innocent creature as you read through the following list of TVP phrases. As you read through the list, think about how an infant might feel if it does not sense that it is cherished or even wanted. Allow yourself to connect with the pain of a helpless creature that is not developed enough to "just know" that its parent cares and is going to do something about its discomfort. Maybe the creature already knows its parent can't or won't.

What's interesting is that these phrases are basically the same monologues that repeat, over and over again, when an adult is having an emotional flashback, and is thrashing about, trying to find the words for how he/she feels.

Tender Vulnerable Part (TVP)
Powerless, stuck, hopeless.

I'm uncomfortable and I can't do anything about it.
I have no choice in what happens to me.
MOTHER* has so much power/I have none.
MOTHER should be here for me.
I've been thrown away (I must be worthless).
I am not valued (I will suffer and die).
MOTHERS should not act this way.
I am not experiencing love.
This is not what I came here for.
My voice isn't heard.
Her thoughts/opinions are stronger than mine.
Her needs are more important than mine.
Misattunement:
She isn't here in the way I need her.
She should be able to attune to my needs.
In this moment (which is my entire reality), depending on others is:
- pointless.
- making things even worse.

I am totally helpless and dependent on her.
Without her I am DEAD.
TERROR
I'm on my own.
FRUSTRATION
How could anybody possibly understand what I'm going through?
I don't have the words.
What did I do to cause this?

CONFUSION (not able to connect logical cause and effect).
There's no use complaining.
HOPELESSNESS
I'm lost.
I don't have any options.
I try, but nothing is working.
I'm miserable.
My choices are nothing without support of MOTHER.
I have no boundaries except the ones MOTHER gives me.
I am powerless without support of MOTHER.
Something is not right here.
Where is the warmth/compassion I so desperately need?
I can't help myself.
My body is not cooperating.
I don't have the control that I need.
I am in pain.
I can't do what I want.
NO ONE is attuning to my needs.
She could help me, but she's not.
Outrage! "What the Bloody Hell?"
BETRAYAL
I don't think I can handle this, the emotions are too much.
RAGE
Overwhelm
I can't regain my composure before the next wave of emotions/bad feelings hit.
I need help regulating my emotions. My nervous system isn't developed enough to do that yet.
I need the help of an attuned, adult brain to develop my ability to regulate my emotions.
DESPAIR

*See note about father, and why he doesn't show up here, at the end of this module.

With awareness and compassion, the shift from powerlessness to understanding can be immediate and profound, and can require nothing more than knowledge and a willingness to empathize with your younger self. Your needs included feeling that you were of primary importance to at least one person, and that you mattered. Your needs were real, but you were not yet sophisticated enough to verbalize or understand them. Neither, apparently, were your parents. Nor were you able to understand the intense physiological reactions your body was having to the stress of not being well-attuned to. If the interruptions in attunement went on for too long, or were not repaired, the infant's system would begin to use a very old trick in order to ensure a different kind of safety and preserve energy: shutdown.

I hope that you can see how valid the HUGE feelings are as responses when one is a very small and vulnerable person with unmet needs. Rage, terror, overwhelm and despair all mark the extreme end of an emotional spectrum that is capable of triggering the body into shutdown, for the sake of safety. Making the connection between what you are hearing inside your head now and the intensely uncomfortable feelings you experienced as a small infant can be the vital first step to eliminating the need for ego defenses and calming the body enough to reconnect with your senses in the present moment. Subsequent steps, which we will talk about in later sections, will involve developing new neural networks in the brain to support creative alternatives to coping defenses.

Rage

Rage is the explosion of out of control emotions (emotional dysregulation). When children are punished for expressing themselves, and abandoned when they need emotional support, they do not learn healthy ways of managing their emotions. They quickly adopt unhealthy ways of hiding and suppressing how they feel in order to preserve whatever approval and acceptance of their parents that they can. Rage is the frightening energy behind Persecutor's power, and can contain any combination of repressed emotions including shame, guilt, fear, sadness, confusion and excitement.

When children grow up in the proximity of adults who can help them learn to work with their emotions, they gain the skills they need to relate to others and themselves in healthy ways. Without models to show them what healthy emotions are, they learn that the world is a frightening place, that it is dangerous to explore or claim their needs and personal limits, and they adapt to avoid the frightening outbursts of the big people they depend upon.

Grief

Sadness and loss in life is inevitable. But if we do not have help understanding and grieving our losses as children, we simply carry them with us until we can. *Sadness signals the need to release something you've been clutching tightly,* Coach tells us. *It is a signal that deserves your attention. And if you learn to recognize it instead of ignore and suppress it, you'll learn that experiencing and honoring your sadness (even if only briefly) leaves you feeling relief - your system lighter and freer of physical constriction and the heaviness you have been carrying for so long.*

Stored grief prevents us from moving forward in our lives. And the kind of grief work we may need to do involves recognizing our lost childhoods and the loving care and attention we needed and didn't get.

Despair

Despair is a collapse of the psyche or the self, and comes at the point of shutdown and dissociation. It is that feeling an infant gets when his or her needs have been unmet for so long that he or she physically collapses in defeat. The switch flips from fight and reach to hide and accept. When this kind of acceptance happens Rescuer offers some solace in the form of an explanation: Maybe I'm just a lost cause. Maybe there is no help for me. Despair is an adaptive response for an infant whose parents may indeed be unavailable, in which case silence and invisibility is the best defense against natural predators. When it becomes the child's primary coping style, he or she then grows up very guarded against pain, doubtful about the reliability of others, and hopelessly self-reliant. In adulthood, shutdown is triggered at the first sign of stress, a response that is silent and automatic. And with the collapse of the self emerges the need for something else to take its place: ego defenses, which we will be talking about soon.

Trusting Ourselves

Terror

Terror is having no idea who or how or what to trust. It's not knowing whether life is actually desirable, or if it is safe to embrace it. Fear, on the other hand, according to Coach, is our friend. She says, *Fear properly channeled yields in-the-moment engagement.* Knowing that we can count on Coach to hold us as we feel our way through the old emotions, and Challenger to keep us grounded in new and relevant knowledge, we can slowly allow our feelings to come back online.

Mistakes

All of us have made mistakes. That's what life is about: Learning from our mistakes and growing. But many of us learned as children that mistakes are not allowed. We did not have the supports we needed in order to learn from them and take that knowledge forward. We learned to hide our mistakes, and with them all our weaknesses – and to be ashamed.

Trusting ourselves has been difficult because the "mistakes" are still hidden, stored in their leaky containers which have served their important purpose, but have actually become fractured and unreliable over time. This means that we respond in stressful situations with the same reflexes we used back then; the reflexes that got us through. But there is so much more for us to choose from. The rigid and mostly unconscious ways we learned to protect ourselves limit us to the same kinds of experiences, and prevent us from relating from our hearts and exploring and expressing ourselves as fully conscious and creative beings.

Ego Defenses

Our automatic reflexes to triggers and stress constitute ego defenses that we adopted to cope with overwhelming emotions in early life. Ego defenses come in many shapes and sizes. They might include withdrawal, doubt, judging, blaming, analyzing, criticizing, or fault-finding. The destructive energies of both Rescuer and Persecutor are ego defenses. The sole purpose of these behaviors is to prevent the closeness of intimacy, which is remembered as a source of great terror and pain for people with insecure attachment. Ego defenses serve as a great smokescreen to keep this assumption well disguised, while helping the person avoid feeling any of their vulnerable emotions: terror, grief, rage, despair.

When we resort to ego defenses instead of staying connected to ourselves in the present we are in essence abandoning ourselves. We're not sure if we can trust ourselves because we've "abandoned ship" in response to triggers and stress from the past. We understandably need to re-establish self-trust.

Staying Attuned to Ourselves

By learning to stay attuned to ourselves and our bodies in the present, we can identify our own behaviors that point to those memories (what we couldn't allow ourselves to "know" back then). This time, with the support of our own inner parents, we can emerge from denial. We can "remember" what happened to us, and give ourselves the care and attention we need to heal and put it behind us. Below are some very clear signals that we can use as requests from our TVP that our attunement and care are needed.

Overwhelm

When I feel overwhelmed, I can understand that I need to pause and parent myself, immediately. Feeling overwhelmed is a message from my TVP that I need care and attention right now. I sometimes forget that the need to pause is real, that my feelings of safety and comfort actually matter.

Hypervigilance

When I notice that I am hypervigilant, I can pause and parent myself. Hypervigilance is one of the signatures of trauma. When we are hypervigilant, the sympathetic nervous system remains activated, even after the danger has passed. Adults with early relational trauma have spent most of their lives hypervigilant, and taking the steps necessary to relax the body and mind is important, but doable work.

Uncomfortable in My Skin

Fear can sometimes feel like a general uncomfortableness. Some people describe it as "uncomfortable in my own skin." If I feel this way, I can pause. Coach can help me to check to see if I'm feeling powerless or helpless inside. If I am, Coach can help me find just the right words: "What do I need to want, what do I need to ask for or what do I need to reach for right now?"

Overwork

Work can be one way to avoid feeling vulnerable emotions. When I notice I am overworking, I can ask myself what I might be avoiding. A healthy life involves balancing work with relaxation and recreation, being in, caring for and enjoying this body right now.

Terror and Boundaries

What if I could trust my own boundaries? What if I could trust myself with my yeses and no's enough so that I could have wealth and abundance alongside people who are struggling financially? What if I could trust that I am worthy and that I can resist the urge to abandon myself in the face of another's needs? If we have learned to live without healthy anger, we unwittingly released the vital energy necessary to distinguish ourselves from others. Their values become our values, our resources become their resources, our crises become their crises, and so on and so forth. With healthy interpersonal boundaries we can finally relax. We will talk about anger and boundaries very soon.

Making Amends

After having repressed our emotions, and having remained in denial so often, and for so long, what would it take for trust to be restored? What force opens the way for the opportunity to mend? The answer is in forgiveness. Making amends with ourselves is a vital part of recovery. In Gary Chapman & Jennifer Thomas's *The Five Languages of Apology*, the authors break down apology into five parts. The first is to express regret. The second is to accept responsibility (which includes accepting that others actually had the control, and we didn't – but that now we do). The third is to make restitution (What can I do to make it right?). The fourth is genuinely repenting (I will try not to do that again). And the fifth is requesting forgiveness (Will you please forgive me?).

For us, making amends will be an ongoing process. Asking for this kind of forgiveness is a huge request, and comes at great cost to the ones we have offended, beginning with ourselves. As Chapman and Thomas say, "When they forgive you, they must give up their desire for justice. They must relinquish their hurt and anger, their feeling of embarrassment or humiliation. They must give up their feeling of rejection and betrayal." If our TVP is willing to forgive, he or she will no longer be demanding justice for what happened. The act of forgiveness naturally releases any hurt and anger, along with feelings of embarrassment and humiliation. Rejection and betrayal fall away like scales. One needs to be truly ready because feelings of hurt and anger can sometimes be more comfortable, familiar and safe. They can also give you a false sense of power. The forgiveness process should not be rushed. You will know when it is time.

The second step of an apology (accepting responsibility) involves taking account of what actually happened. So often we don't even allow ourselves to know, so this may be a significant amount of work in and of itself. Once you can allow yourself to "know" what happened, you are well on your way. Then you can take responsibility for your part, and let go of the rest.

There have been many consequences for our trauma-tinged choices and behaviors. We have sabotaged relationships in order to avoid repeating the loss we felt as powerless infants. We have used ego defenses instead of feeling our feelings and reaching out for the connections we so desire and need. In our efforts to avoid repeating the ancient losses, we have drawn into our lives people who have not been able to give us what we need. And if they had, we would not have been able to receive it.

Attraction

Breaking through our denial and creating an inner environment in which it is safe to know what we know and feel what we feel allows us to begin to trust ourselves again. As inconceivable as it sounds, intimacy has functioned as a powerful trigger for you. The presence of unprocessed memories, their associated core beliefs, and powerful body memories make us triggerable in relation to the prospect of the sweet closeness that was interrupted in childhood (maybe even at birth). As long as these memories remain in exile, we are prone to emotional flashbacks and regression when faced with the prospect of getting close again.

We will also continue to be attracted to people who help us recognize (like it or not) the dynamics of the unresolved trauma that has been installed in the mind and body by our upbringing.

When you notice an attraction for someone, whether it is platonic or romantic, it is an excellent time to slow down and just notice, while resisting any urges to act. It is impossible to know, at first, whether the attraction is based on your unresolved emotions and the monumental urge to repeat your traumas until you resolve them, or if this new person is actually going to become someone trusted and cherished over time. Stay conscious and connected with your wisest self, consult with your Inner Parents, and take your time. There really is no rush.

How many times have you followed an uncanny attraction toward another person, only to discover that the relationship was much more complicated than you could have ever imagined?

What were those first feelings? What were the early signals?

Feeling over-excited? Feeling swept off your feet (hoping someone else will carry your weight)?

Doubting or dismissing your own observations?

Separating from your body (blocking emotions)?

Running and re-running old tapes?

Feeling overwhelmed, powerless, confused?

Pause. Check and re-check with your inner parents. Breathe. Take another deep breath. There is no need to rush here. What do you want? What is it you would really like here? Connection? Cool. What would that look like? What are the qualities of the connection you desire? Is that what you are experiencing here?

The object is to return to a fully relaxed and grounded state as many times as necessary. Only from a relaxed state can you take in new information from the present moment and respond appropriately instead of out of deeply ingrained patterns that you adopted from a different time.

This is the end of Module 3, and what is intended to be the first half of this course. Take a few days to absorb this material. Make focused attention activities part of your daily routine. This means you get 10-20 minutes of time dedicated to YOU. Use any activity that is interesting to you, and that can successfully take your attention away from an urge or compulsion to talk disparagingly to yourself, or any other compulsive activity you engage in to avoid feeling emotions. Any of the assignments in the Module Review or on the Focused Attention Activities List can be used as focused attention activities.

Module 3 Review – TVP Shifts to Creator

Activities

Watch the TED Talk by Stuart Brown on play:

https://www.ted.com/talks/stuart_brown_says_play_is_more_than_fun_it_s_vital

Answer the questions about play and pleasure on the Play and Pleasure worksheet (pg 86).

Wrap yourself in a soft blanket and listen to soft music until you fall asleep.

Watch small children play. Join them if you want.

Mourning in Giraffe (pg 88)

Read: A Note About Dad (pg 90)

Discussions on Play and Pleasure

Stuart Brown is a researcher on the important topic of play. In this TED Talk, he discusses play. If you haven't already, please watch the video and answer the questions below.

https://www.ted.com/talks/stuart_brown_says_play_is_more_than_fun_it_s_vital

1) What is your "play history"?

2) What is play to you?

3) What feelings accompany pleasure for you?

4) How do you integrate fun and play with others in your life?

Mourning in Giraffe

This is a process to heal ourselves concerning a choice we made in the past that we now regret. It is a way of acknowledging our regret and of empathizing with ourselves so we can grow beyond our past limitations.

Perhaps we may think we are "correcting the situation" or "making up" for a past mistake by continuing to blame ourselves and prolonging our sense of guilt and shame. Yet, as St. Frances de Sales wrote, "Those who are fretted by their own failings will not correct them. All profitable corrections come from a calm and peaceful mind."

There is a belief in our culture that the suffering of the perpetrator makes up for the loss that victims undergo – an eye for an eye. As a practitioner of NVC, if I lose an eye as a consequence of your behavior, I know my deep need for empathy, compassion, safety, etc., will not be met by your offering me either your self-judgment or your eye. I will be able to receive what I need from you only after you have taken the much harder path of truly mourning the choices you have made. The healing between us will happen when I can hear the depth of your mourning and you can offer me the depth of empathy that I need.

Use the following to mourn a choice you made in the past that you now regret.

a. Observation: what I said or did in the past that I now regret

b. Self-judgments: what I think of myself for having done or said (a)

c. Current feelings and needs: translate self-judgments into feelings and needs

d. Empathy for myself: determine what need I was trying to fulfill when I chose to take the action or say the words I now regret

e. Current request of myself:

Aware of my current feelings and unfulfilled needs (c), I would like to address my needs (d) in the following manner:

This exercise comes from *Nonviolent Communication Companion Workbook*, by Lucy Leu, pg 124-25.

Notes: What about Dad?

In this course, I use what might seem like erratic treatment of pronouns. Bear with me, there is some method to this madness.

We – men and women alike – were all children and we all experienced that warm physical connection with our mother. At the very least, we were protected by the design and physiology of the womb so that all our needs were met, effortlessly. Mother's body does an excellent job of physically buffering the child and putting its needs first, whether she is stressed, malnourished, or abused. That is, before birth. So my intention is to include both "he" and "she" when it comes to the experience of the offspring and its perspective as a fetus and newborn. But when it comes to the adult parent that the stress or trauma is associated with, I am using "she" across the board. At this point, the bond with mother is primary, the bond with the father is at a very different stage.

This is not to hold the mother entirely responsible. Nothing could be further from the truth. It is the responsibility of the tribe to support women in their childbearing years and to help raise small children, though this relationship and responsibility has been all but erased in our society. The mother is who carries the child during gestation. There is no getting around this. The severing of that connection in violent and unconscious ways at birth is an important contributor to early relational trauma.

The father's direct contribution comes in later, when the child is able to leave that warm womb-place of the mother. For biological reasons the father's role during pregnancy and in those first months is to provide a safe environment, to support the mother, and to guard against predators during this vulnerable, transitional time. This is not to diminish the importance of the father-infant bond or the father-pre-infant bond. But the stresses and traumas that TVP is telling us about (through the voices I hear from clients who are in flashback) are about the rage and terror originating from the separation from mother. The bond with father is secondary until the later developmental stages and isn't as directly or obviously involved in the co-dependent stage of development.

Many of the ways we abuse ourselves – the ego defenses we pick up – are internalized father voices, and are reflective of father wounds. But they take root in very different ways, depending on the quality of the bond and the safety we felt in the time between conception and 6 months. In this course I refer to these unresolved stresses and traumas in terms of how the infant/baby's body responded, whether as a way to cope with lack of attunement or prolonged separations (whether they are physical or energetic), or a chronic triggered reaction from the mother in response to the child's vulnerability and neediness.

Module 3 Quiz 1:

1) (True or False) For children, complaining is natural and adaptive. It's a way to express important needs.

2) The following examples of inner dialogue characterize the voice of the Tender Vulnerable Part.

   A. Confusion (Not able to connect logical cause and effect).
   B. I am not valued (TERROR – I will suffer and die).
   C. I don't know what to do/where to start.
   D. This is never going to get better.
   E. All of the above.

3) The following are examples of strategies that infants and small children often use when their home does not feel safe to them and emotional needs for attunement are not being adequately met.

   A. Trying to be invisible in attempts to not be noticed
   B. Disconnecting from uncomfortable feelings
   C. Taking responsibility for things we have no control over
   D. Focusing on and tending to others' needs
   E. Denial, cynicism, self-betrayal
   F. All of the above
   G. B & D above

4) Novelty can be either a threat or a source of pleasure, depending on:

   A. Existence of body memories.
   B. Whether or not you felt safe as a child.
   C. Whether or not it triggers defensive response patterns and increases hypervigilance.
   D. All of the above.

Module 4 - Rescuer Shifts to Coach

Solution in the Face of an Impossible Dilemma

In childhood, Rescuer offered up a creative "solution" in the face of an impossible dilemma. This creative solution developed in response to unmitigated stress during infancy or childhood, which effectively helped you regain a sense of equilibrium then, but it is causing you problems now.

Rescuer energy steps in without first asking, doing whatever she can to make you more comfortable (protect you from uncomfortable feelings) in the moment. She is extremely creative, and the solutions she creates are so effective that it's almost impossible to see through them when they emerge. They're not logical, and they're not obvious, but you can learn to recognize them. They are ingenious, and they were necessary, but now the cost is greater than the momentary comfort they bring.

One of the things that make the Drama Triangle so toxic is the unhealthy bond between TVP and Rescuer based on shame. In the Drama Triangle game, TVP agrees to remain dependent and powerless to honor Rescuer.

The Shift

When Rescuer shifts into the feminine energy of Coach, she empowers TVP. She offers support in recognizing and tending to emotions, so that TVP can figure out what he or she wants and needs, and make that powerful shift to Creator. Coach asks the questions necessary to connect TVP with her desires and needs and re-engage trust in life. She doesn't require that Creator remain powerless and dependent on her, but rather offers necessary attunement, nurture and support so that Creator can feel confident and capable. She says things like, *What feelings are alive in this moment? I'll be right here for you while you move through that feeling. It's okay. That's completely normal. Just notice it. It's not here to stay.* Then she might check in with us and ask, *What's going on now? What do you need? What is the creative desire here? How can I help you figure that out?* She is able to attune to our needs and compassionately hold us while we feel what we feel and know what we know.

Coach plays a maternal role, though she is likely to be very different from your mother. Her role is to acknowledge the validity of your inner child's experience. It's her task to pass on the instinct of self-valuing, self-nurturing, not to "mother" you for the rest of your life. In this way, she teaches you to trust yourself.

Working with Challenger, Coach takes us by the hand and helps us discover thoughts that bring feelings of empowerment and relief. Then, when the body is calm and unguarded, we are more likely to recognize and accept real help and support from the outside world when it shows up.

Coach as Inner Feminine

Coach, in her larger, universal essence, is the Inner Feminine. Inner Feminine is Pure Receptivity. And each of us has her essence within us. She is flow and light. She is Life Force. She is Deep Radiance. For her, there is no need to control anything. She just IS. She is the heart, yearning; the depth of desire. But not from a sense of powerlessness. She draws to herself that which she desires and opens to receive what is good.

Framework for Coach as Inner Feminine

Notice the emotions, including guilt and shame.

Check to see if you are Rescuing yourself (and stop).

Ask Rescuer to switch to Coach who offers compassion.

Have compassion for yourself, knowing that your rescue strategies were extremely helpful in the past but that now there are other options.

Forgive yourself for using such costly tactics in the past. They were your best options then (grief work may be necessary before you are ready for this).

Ask what is needed to help TVP move toward relief.

Ask what subtle adjustments need to be made. She might say things like:

I'm sure this is no fun. Let me just cradle you here until you feel better. Tell me, just how frustrated are you?

How lonely?

How scared?

How overwhelmed?

How tired?

How discouraged?

I'm right here with you. Take your time. It's perfectly safe to feel and notice the nuance of these emotions. They will pass. You have support now. Don't try to control them anymore. Feel and notice them. Breathe. Resist the urge to do anything right now. All important decisions and actions can wait until you are calm and grounded. Let the world wait. Take your time so that your response will be conscious and wise.

Presence Transforms

The role of Coach is to help us accept and express on the outside more of what we are experiencing on the inside. This task requires humility, courage, and willingness to change. It takes time, consistency and patience to attune to our inner states, and then to learn what to do about them. But it is the only way we can be our authentic selves with others. You will see. All of the effort you invest in knowing and accepting yourself as you truly are will pay off.

Coach offers support in re-connecting us with our emotional instincts. *Feelings are real, she tells us. They are not ideas that can be turned off. And they are not a threat to us. They give us invaluable information about what we like and don't like, about what we want more of and what isn't working for us.*

What happens when we reconnect with our feelings and emotions?

Our responses to other people have become habitual, compulsive and ingrained. Instead of feeling our feelings and claiming our space in the world, we have been what others needed us to be, and we have survived. Now that we are aware, we can reclaim our fully embodied selves and destinies as our very own and thrive. *What we want and need matters,* Coach tells us, *and just knowing that offers us a freshness of response, a spontaneity that wasn't there before. But to achieve this we have to accept ourselves as emotional beings. As we do, we see the value of studying and developing an awareness of our physical reactions, the signals our bodies have been giving us all along that we've been ignoring. When that happens, and we recognize that we are afraid, we make the necessary adjustments in order to be safe. When that happens and we recognize that we are angry, we honor ourselves enough to speak up about what does and does not work for us, and then follow through so that we are once again living in integrity with ourselves and our most essential needs and limits.*

Feelings are neither positive nor negative, but they are essential to our health and well-being. According to Coach, *they are simply your body's way of communicating its needs – not vastly different from the information that an infant, before he or she learns to speak, offers its caretakers. Essentially, constriction signals that we are afraid, and fear, when we give it appropriate attention compels us to seek safety and comforting; heat signals anger, which helps us identify our boundaries and how we and our needs are different from those around us; lethargy and heaviness signal sadness, which informs us about what we have truly valued, and signal the need to slow down and let go of what we've been holding on to that is no longer alive or truly serving us; pleasure tells us about what enhances us, and what we want more of.*

As you learn that your emotions are part of your highly sophisticated inner navigational system, it will be easier to maintain a cooperative, balanced internal environment, and you will be more able to notice and utilize your emotions as they arise. As you grow in your ability to tolerate and use your emotions to inform your choices, you will be less susceptible to manipulation and the emotional chaos of others.

This is the end of Module 4, and what is intended to be the fourth week of this course. Take a few days to absorb this material. If you would like to talk to Toni, send her an e-mail. If her schedule allows, she will gift you with 20-30 minutes of her focused attention. Continue to gift yourself with YOUR attention. Just 10-20 minutes a day will make all the difference in the world. Or you could try 10 minutes early in the day and 20 minutes later on. Don't skip it even if you have to be creative, or do it imperfectly. It's really up to you. See what works best. Any of the activities below can be used to help you focus your attention.

Module 4 Review –Rescuer Shifts to Coach

Schedule: e-mail Toni at toniarahman@hotmail.com for a virtual appointment to experience being held in empathic Coach Energy.

Activities:

Mother Work (pg 98)
Significant Traumas & Betrayals (pg 100)
Making Amends – Complete the Worksheet (pg 102)
Write a letter to yourself from your Inner Feminine (pg 104)

Mother Work

Three things I love about my mother:

Three things I hate about her:

Three wishes for her:

Three resentments I have toward her:

When comparing myself with my mother, I can see how we have the following in common:

Significant Traumas and Betrayals

Make a list of all the significant betrayals you have experienced in your life, whether you were the person betrayed or the person who betrayed someone else.

After making your list, journal on the following questions.

- What similarities are there between these traumas?
- What were the circumstances?
- How did I feel in each betrayal or trauma?
- What beliefs, values, assumptions and expectations have I formed about myself and about the world as a result of all these traumas and betrayals?
- How does my earliest trauma replay over and over in my life?
- What dramas seem to play over and over?
- What was unfinished about each of the trauma/betrayal experiences?
- What do I need to do to finish each of these experiences?
- Look at your life drama to see what isn't finished. Examine each event or betrayal to see what you need to do to complete it.

What Do You Need To Make Amends For?

After having repressed our emotions, and having remained in denial so often, and for so long, what would it take to trust ourselves again?

What were the consequences of your regretted behavior?

Along with forgiveness, any desire for justice is instantly released along with hurt and anger, feeling of embarrassment, humiliation, rejection and betrayal. If TVP is willing to forgive, rejection and betrayal fall away like scales. One needs to be truly ready because feelings of hurt and anger can sometimes be more comfortable, familiar and safe. The forgiveness process should not be rushed, and might need to be done more than once. You will know when you are ready.

Would you be willing to make amends to yourself?

1) The first step is to express regret.

2) The second step is to accept responsibility (taking account of what actually happened).

3) The third step is to make restitution (What can I do to make it right?).

4) The fourth step is genuinely repenting (I will try not to do that again).

5) The fifth step is requesting forgiveness (Will you please forgive me?).

These steps are those suggested by Gary Chapman & Jennifer Thomas in *The Five Languages of Apology*

Letter from Your Inner Feminine (example):

My Beloved One,

I adore you. You are a child of God. You have my full permission to be all you came here to be. Take your time. Take all the time you need. I am strong enough to support you, while you explore who you are and what you will do next and next and next. How precious you are to me. I can't wait to see what you next discover about yourself, your strengths, your yet unexplored gifts and qualities and potentials. I give you permission and my blessing to indulge in pleasure, to explore the world, inner and outer, to be great, to be vulnerable, to be playful, to be a beginner - to be exactly who you are now. I am holding this space and time for you while you do this very important work. Go ahead. Let yourself feel your emotions. It is safe to be in your body now. Listen to what it tells you. I will offer you guidance and direction through your sensory experience and I encourage you to enter the full expression of your deepest self, from this moment onward. You are enough. You are so precious to me. I love you so.

I will be here for you always.

Your Inner Feminine

Write your letter from your Inner Feminine here.

Module 4 Quiz 1:

1) The following are examples of Rescuer Talk
   A. I must have done something wrong (trying to figure out what it is).
   B. It's my fault (I'm suffering because of my bad choices) obviously.
   C. I've allowed myself to be manipulated, so I must deserve this.
   D. There is something wrong with me (I'm flawed somehow).
   E. All of the above

2) (True or False) The most important function of Rescuer is to protect us from uncomfortable feelings.

3) The following are examples of things Coach might say:

   A. What feelings are alive in this moment?
   B. I'll be right here for you while you move through that feeling.
   C. It's okay. That's completely normal.
   D. Just notice it. It's not here to stay.
   E. What do you need? How can I help you figure that out?
   F. All of the above

4) The Drama Triangle Game is responsible for people feeling that they give all the time and never receive because:

   A. To win the Drama Triangle Game one has to become the victim.
   B. To get what one truly wants one has to be willing to ask, and the Drama Triangle game fosters an environment in which members never directly ask for what they want and need.
   C. When one manipulates others into anticipating their wants and needs, they rarely get what they truly desire.
   D. The game keeps people feeling guarded and so on edge that they cannot relax enough to receive or to trust the motives of givers.
   E. All of the above

5) Which of the following statements would Coach never say?

   A. Feelings are real. They are not ideas that can be turned off.
   B. Emotions are physical manifestations of energy, uniting body and mind and bringing them to the moment.

C. Love is the expression of positive emotions in the moment.
D. Love is emotional energy flowing rightly. It is the full range of emotions expressed appropriately, in the moment, honestly, directly.

Module 5 - Persecutor Shifts to Challenger

Solution in the Face of an Impossible Dilemma

Though it is less obvious to us, Persecutor also serves as a creative "solution" in the face of impossible dilemma. Just like Rescuer, Persecutor steps in to maintain a sense of equilibrium, and also at great cost.

We know that Persecutor is in play when we are blaming ourselves, when we are calling ourselves names, or when we are using terms such as "always," "never," or "obviously." Persecutor talks down at us, as if we were unable to learn and should be punished for our mistakes.

Persecutor Energy is abusive. But it also alerts us to very real needs that we can attend to if we know how. The first thing we need to do is pause. Take a few deep breaths. When we notice Persecutor showing up and dominating our inner environment, we can immediately acknowledge our need to discharge the energy of an emotion. It might be anger, but it's just as possible that it is shame, vulnerability, rejection or fear, and our automatic response is "protecting" us from reliving the original pain of this emotion.

Blaming, shaming, criticizing, ridiculing – these are all just smokescreens, causing so much static that they cover up and distract us from feelings of vulnerability, fear and worry. But since they are abusive, they need to be recognized and shifted. We can use them as red flags from now on, telling us that we have some vulnerabilities or other unmet needs. These needs might include:

Basic safety.
Patience and lovingkindness.
Encouragement.
Unconditional love and acceptance.
Touch and affection.
Support in learning social and emotional skills.
Support in learning to regulate emotions.

The Shift

What would happen, if after noticing that we have been abusing ourselves, we asked Persecutor to make the gentle pivot necessary to play the role of Challenger instead? The intense energy of Persecutor would shift to the still strong but benevolent masculine energy of Challenger, whose job it is to hold us accountable, but to do it without abuse, to do it with the goal of supporting our growth and learning. In the role of Challenger, we can use this energy to help TVP to reconnect with his/her desires and to help him/her understand what steps are needed to reach them.

Challenger plays a paternal role, though he may be quite different from your father. His role is to teach you how to express your heart as he initiates you into the world of relationships with others. It's his task to pass on the instinct of friendship. He embodies the instinctive ability to relate appropriately to others, teaching loyalty, companionship, sharing, and fairness.

Challenger as Inner Masculine

Challenger in his larger, universal essence is the Inner Masculine. Inner Masculine is Imperturbable Consciousness. And each of us has his essence within us. He is Structure. He gets things done. His is the ability to remain present through thick and thin. He is larger than criticism. He is not jerked around by our always-changing thoughts and emotions. He is more aware of us than we are. He takes us deeper. He penetrates illusion to fill us with consciousness and help us claim our depth.

As Challenger helps us untangle the snarl of confusion and cut through the fog of the emotional flashback, we receive insights and make connections that weren't possible in the chaos of the Drama Triangle. Challenger works closely with Coach to help us identify our immediate needs and desires and works toward identifying the immediate steps that need to be taken next.

Framework for Challenger as Inner Masculine

So far, we have learned that we have tender vulnerable feelings, and we have devised ingenious and almost foolproof ways to protect ourselves from them. There are many signs to watch for so that we can check to see if we are avoiding our feelings. Though we have the option of moving through life suppressing and ignoring our feelings, we give up so much when we do. Below is a basic outline for assessing and shifting the tone of our inner environment.

Questions Challenger might ask in order to hold us accountable, while reestablishing safety:

What is your intention in this situation?
What needs to be done in order to take charge of your life?
What's real here?
In what ways has this (unwanted behavior/automatic response) actually served

you? (working as a way to escape, shutting down emotions, self-criticism, etc.)

How can you discharge the energy of this emotion without beating up on yourself or hurting someone else?

What need does this behavior/attitude/belief fulfill?

In what ways does it need to be honored?

What is it telling you?

How can it be used for good?

Challenger helps connect you to an appreciation for yourself for having survived the intense experiences that made you concoct this complex but effective survival tool. It was necessarily complex because if it hadn't been, you would have been able to see through it, and it wouldn't have worked!

Knowledge IS Power

Understanding the Cognitive Effects of Trauma

A feature of early relational trauma is that we have trouble verbalizing things in a logical, linear manner because things in our brains are still stored chaotically, without yet being processed. Also, the connections between cause and effect are compromised, making it difficult to see the connections between past and present and our choices and their natural outcomes. If you can understand this about yourself, you will stop judging yourself for your difficulty in communicating under certain circumstances, and for feeling delayed in particular ways. As you work through your trauma you will gradually be more coherent and at ease in your communication and the connections will become more clear. You are not stupid and there is nothing "wrong" with you. You do have some catch-up work to do. There is no shame in this.

Understanding the Physiological Effects of Trauma

There are many physiological effects of trauma. One is the set of primitive protective reflexes our body utilizes as a result of prolonged stress. I provide a link at the end of this module where you can explore this more if you like. Another is the cutting off of awareness to our feelings. Numbing out may have been a reliable refuge for you. Thank goodness for the body's ability to do that. Little by little your senses can come back online. And when they do, they may not – at first – be exactly comfortable. Allow them to come back when they are ready. Take steps to make it safe for them to do so, but don't make yourself wrong for feeling numb.

Understanding Shame

Shame is an important area to examine with the help of Challenger energy and should be something you return to from time to time so that old assumptions and beliefs can be examined in the light of your current, adult, ever-evolving understandings and values. Healthy shame keeps you accountable to yourself and your values. Toxic shame is a favorite tool of Persecutor and other abusers. You can tell them apart by identifying their focus. Healthy shame focuses on specific behaviors and their appropriateness with respect to your values, while toxic shame constantly questions your "worth" or "acceptableness" as a person.

Distinguishing Between Nurturing and Sexual Touch

Research has shown that confusing sexual energy with nurturing energy is a feature of disorganized attachment and early relational trauma (80-90% of people seeking therapy and therapists have experienced this). A number of features of the Drama Triangle are responsible for this. One is the unhealthy bond between the Adult Rescuer (male or female) and the TVP, based on shame. In some ways, this unhealthy alliance feels similar to romantic partnership and therefore results in the same damaging symptoms as actual sexual abuse. You may recall that Rescuer needs TVP to be dependent upon him or her, requiring that TVP not mature and individuate in a healthy manner. At some level TVP agrees to do this, and the bond is forged, a secret alliance that gives them a sense of timeless but twisted connectedness and intimacy.

The other confounding thing is that people with disorganized attachment have associated intimacy with imminent danger. For them, arousal and desire can be extremely triggering. Nonetheless, our need to touch and be touched is real. Our need to yearn and desire is valid, and our need for closeness and intimacy will be a feature of our existence as long as we live.

Education, time and experimentation is necessary to help us formulate the questions we need to ask in order to address this confusion around sexual and nurturing touch and the associations we have developed with intimacy, shame and pleasure. With the help of Coach and Challenger, we can safely bring these unhealthy dynamics to light so they don't just continue to swirl around, unexamined, in our energy field, and out in the world. Apparently, we are in good company.

Though it is not obvious on people's "outsides," the symptoms of developmental trauma are pervasive and real. As we heal and achieve greater and greater levels of healthy individuation, our sense of what is sexual and what is nurturing becomes much more clear.

Understanding Boundaries

Boundaries are systematically discouraged, punished and obliterated in environments where the Drama Triangle is being played out. Not having strong boundaries and needing to establish them later in life is completely understandable and nothing to be ashamed about. Having healthy boundaries allows a person to be in the presence of another while simultaneously maintaining a unique, separate but connected, living, vibrant, authentic, whole self.

If you notice yourself spending money or time or energy that you don't feel you have, this is an indication that you are experiencing boundary failure or lack of boundaries. If you notice yourself taking on the negative moods of the people around you, or unable to maintain a positive state when you are with certain people, this is a signal that you need to do some emotional work to strengthen your unique identity and your boundaries. Identifying your boundaries is actually figuring out what is okay with you and what isn't. And believe it or not, that is also the basic function of healthy anger. We will talk more about anger later on.

Understanding Urges and Compulsions

The ego defenses that we develop in childhood can also be thought of as urges or compulsions. Because these responses have become hardwired and automatic, we sometimes need to develop strategies to overcome them. Resisting an urge can often keep us from going into a full-fledged emotional flashback. Consider adopting the four-step plan on the next page to deal with compulsions and urges.

First, it's important to remember that urges (including urges to rescue, blame ourselves, binge, self-harm, etc.) are things that our BRAIN learned how to do as a once-adaptive response to stress. Compulsions and urges are the behaviors that both Rescuer and Persecutor had us do so many times to distract us from overwhelming emotions. As adults, here is what we can do instead of yielding to the urge or compulsion.

Four-Step Approach to Responding to Urges and Compulsions

1) Name the experience (just naming it helps reduce the stress).

I am aware that I'm having a compulsion to _____.

I'm aware that I'm having this sensation of _____.

I'm aware that I'm having the emotion of _____ because of _____.

check my phone b/c of my desire to know if someone txted me/ = thought of me

2) Frame the behavior and identify its function in the past.

This makes sense because this is what my brain learned to do when I felt powerless, etc.

or

It's just my younger scared self; she has a real need, and I am interested in identifying and tending to it.

or

This is happening because I need: *sense of belonging/ ↓ loneliness)*
- a sense of relief.
- a way to escape.
- a way to express my voice.
- etc.

3) Ask: How would I like this to go differently?

Example: I see myself being able to excuse myself briefly (to check in with myself) instead of pretending that I'm engaged in a conversation (but I'm really shutting down and waiting for it to be over).

4) Concentrate on something other than the urge (Focused Attention).

(REPEAT AS NECESSARY)

Focused attention actually re-wires the brain (when you can successfully resist the urge). This activity through which you focus your attention can be anything meaningful and productive that requires your attention. A list of Focused Attention activities is included in the Course Activities and Assignments Section.

Modified from Alsana Treatment Center for Eating Disorders
Also check out this resource: URGE911.com

Understanding Your Sphere of Responsibility

Growing up under the spell of the Drama Triangle, we often got confusing signals about responsibility and control. We were made to feel guilty for someone else's pain. We were made to feel responsible for other people's feelings and behaviors. And as all children do, we took responsibility when bad things happened to us. We didn't know any better, and it helped us feel like we had at least some control, even when we had so little. That is why it comes as such a surprise, as an adult, to learn how little control you actually have over all of life. Letting go of things you have no control over, then, becomes a major part of your emotional work. Though it's not easy, it has a tremendous payoff. I've included a list of things we actually have some control over at the end of this module. The list is shorter than you might think.

Understanding the Power and Potential of Social Engagement

It can sometimes be useful to reach out and ask someone you trust to listen while you talk. Asking them to reflect back to you what you are saying can add to your awareness of what your TVP is feeling and needing. Their experience of you, if it feels compassionate and feels true, can expand your knowledge and understanding of your needs and desires. Know that this can and will bring up things for the other person too, but relationship can also be a place where the two of you experiment and learn together how to better stay in the here and now instead of the past, stuck in reliving trauma drama and projection. If there is no one to reach out to, you might be able to benefit from listening to safe others in an anonymous setting such as Al-Anon. At an Al-Anon or Adult Children of Alcoholics meeting you can experience what it feels like to be received anonymously and learn a lot just by watching and listening to others.

Understanding Emotion Language

Though you probably didn't learn this as a child, there are fairly universal maps to understanding emotional language. It's not too late to do that now. For instance if I notice myself criticizing, comparing, blaming, or judging myself or someone else, I can take note. I can then pledge to have a "sit down" with myself, ASAP. It's kind of like what GOOD parents do when they see their child doing something that is harmful or unhealthy. Once you have your own attention, take the opportunity, as soon as possible, to tend to it.

"Tending to it" might involve writing down the words that have invaded your peace of mind. If they are not friendly and reassuring, or if they are condescending or shaming, they need your attention sooner, rather than later. If they are tender vulnerable feelings it is important that you make it a priority to take some time to do your emotional work. You can learn to care for all of your emotions in appropriate ways so that their respective information and energy can be utilized and discharged. In the list below I include literal emotions as well as behaviors that can cue you in to a "forbidden" or suppressed emotion.

What Your Emotions Are Telling You About Your Needs

Anger – Examine, adjust, or establish boundaries or personal limits:
> When there is some kind of breach in the boundary that needs to be repaired,
> When I don't have confidence that I have adequate boundaries in place, or
> When I have been living without healthy boundaries, possibly for a long time.

Rage – Check with Challenger to see what is real, and what needs to happen to establish safety. Check in with Coach for support in feeling and releasing.

Shame – Check with Challenger to see what is real, and what needs to happen to establish integrity. May need to grieve.

Guilt – Check with Challenger to see what is real, and what needs to happen to establish integrity. May need to grieve.

Criticizing – Check to see if I'm either scared of something and not admitting it, or I'm angry and resentful.

Resenting – Have a "sit down" with myself and check for early anger or tender vulnerable feelings.

Blaming – Have a "sit down" with myself and check for early anger or tender vulnerable feelings.

Judging – Have a "sit down" with myself and check for early anger or tender vulnerable feelings.

Fear – Check with Challenger to see what is real, and what needs to happen to establish safety.

Terror – Check with Challenger to see what is real, and what needs to happen to establish safety. Check in with Coach for support in feeling and releasing.

Suspicion – Check with Challenger to see what is real, and what needs to happen to tend to boundaries.

Complaining – Pause, listen to myself with compassion and check to see what I've been afraid to ask for.

Shoulding – Pause and write it out. Sometimes indicates fear, but is often more complex. Shoulds can be transformed into feelings and needs.

Attraction – Slow waaay down. Check with Challenger to see what is real, and what needs to happen to establish safety. Check in with Coach for support in feeling and releasing. Identify and take back projections.

Overexcited – Check with Challenger to see what is real, and what needs to happen to establish safety. Check in with Coach for support in feeling and releasing.

Worry – Check with Challenger to see what is real, and what needs to happen to establish safety. Check in with Coach for support in feeling and releasing.

Vulnerability – Check with Challenger to see what is real, and what needs to happen to establish safety.

Sadness – Check in with Coach for support in feeling and releasing.

Grief – Check in with Coach for support in feeling and releasing.

Comparing – Have a "sit down" with myself and check for early anger or tender vulnerable feelings.

Numbing – Check with Challenger to see what needs to happen to establish safety. Check in with Coach for support in connecting with feelings.

Overwhelm – Check in with Coach for support in feeling and releasing. Check with Challenger to see what is real, and what needs to happen to establish safety.

Understanding the Nature of Mistakes

Everybody makes mistakes. Life is about making mistakes and learning from them. In order for you to know that you want something, you must have had plenty of life experiences that have helped you know what you do not want. Thus, mistakes provide you with vital information.

Understanding and Calling Out Social Programming

Society has names for people they consider to be too self-absorbed. I, for one, think we should be curious about this seeming aversion to caring and advocating for oneself. Chances are, we have met people who seemed to have no capacity to consider the feelings of others (we call them all kinds of things: narcissists, sociopaths, predators, etc.). And we have probably been hurt by them, and would never want to be anything like them. The thing is, even they are not exempt from this rule: Those who do not take responsibility for their own feelings and needs, are going to have a hard time with the expressed limits and needs of others. But when we don't speak up for ourselves, who really stands to benefit? Name calling (selfish, narcissistic, self-absorbed) is a way to make people feel ashamed, and shaming is a form of manipulation and abuse. And when we internalize it, we abuse ourselves in the same way. By the same token, when we apply this label to someone else with a broad stroke, we are doing what Persecutor does best: Judging. Judging, remember, is an ego defense against feeling our own vulnerable feelings. The better strategy is to get off the Drama Triangle and ditch our knee-jerk reactions, and to become completely unashamed to matter to ourselves.

Working with Coach, Challenger can release Creator to go after what he or she really wants and needs in every situation, every relationship. This is not "selfishness" but a refreshing sense of self responsibility that allows us to be completely present for every person and every task in our life as it emerges.

Another myth is that of "spoiling" children. The idea of spoiling implies that something is permanently altered in a negative way, indulged foolishly with a permanent negative result. It is a value judgment. And the idea is preposterous. Research on attachment shows unequivocally that babies who are securely attached cry less, are less clingy, and have fewer stress hormones than babies whose caretakers showed a poor level of attunement to the child's needs; who have been ridiculed, left alone to deal with their feelings of overwhelm, or felt consistently unsupported. "Spoiling" is a word that a stressed and fearful parent uses because their child's needs are terrifying to them due to their own unresolved early childhood experiences.

Don't worry. With Challenger's help the shaming that happens with words like "spoiled" or "selfish" can be quickly redirected.

Understanding Neuroplasticity

Thank GOD and Nature that our brains remain malleable throughout adulthood, and we can have experiences as adults that correct, repair, and "finish" the things that didn't fully develop in childhood and infancy. Connecting and "feeling attuned to" are normal parts of a healthy life and you are normal for wanting more of that. Know that "more of that" is indeed available. Keep reaching, and then allow it to come to you.

Understanding the Window of Tolerance

Follow your comfort level. Good therapy helps you learn that you do have some control over how you experience emotions. It is not necessary to suffer to recover from trauma. If you equate therapy with overwhelming feelings and re-traumatization, I would suggest that you find a different therapist.

Interpersonal Anger

In our first relationships, we learn what we can and can't think, feel, speak, or want. We actually learn, very early on, what is and is not allowed.

— Toni Rahman, *Being In My Body: What You Might Not Have Known About Trauma, Dissociation & The Brain*

Healthy Boundaries and their Relationship with Healthy Anger

We can count on other people to offer us challenges. They give us the opportunity to practice taking two deep breaths (or a nap) before responding. Other people may believe that they are entitled to our attention this very moment, but the truth is, we can best respond (for the best result of ALL involved) when we are not "reacting" to their emergency, but rather from a calm and resourced place to give what we have to give and do what we need to do without sacrificing ourselves and our peace of mind, rushing, or diving into their crisis with them.

Anger protects our personal territory against real invasion. And it alerts us when there are imbalances that need correcting. It is the appropriate response when another adult person feels that they are entitled to our immediate attention or our resources. We might have a history of feeling that we have to jump when they call us, or share with them beyond our capacity or desire. We might feel like they have more power over us than we like. This is an indication that we have given our power away, and that we need to reclaim it. To do this, we may need help reconnecting with our boundaries, or healthy anger.

When Anger Is Appropriate

Though we really cannot know for sure what another person thinks or feels, when we have evidence (however subtle) that another person is violating a boundary or invading our territory in some way, it is normal for us to feel something, and to allow that feeling into our consciousness. It is there to help keep us safe and relating with others in healthy ways.

Anger Misconceptions

If you grew up in an environment where the Drama Triangle was alive and well, you probably got the wrong idea about anger. Anger is not the explosion of a temper tantrum. It is not scary, abusive or irresponsible. It doesn't involve acting out in ways that harm our most cherished relationships, disrespect others, embarrass us, or sabotage our deepest values. That is rage you are thinking about.

Emotional Dysregulation

If you associate anger with danger or destruction, the adults in your life did not know how to regulate their emotions. They suppressed the energy of their emotions, neglected their own needs past their breaking point, and then they exploded. That is why so many in our society mistake rage (waiting until anger is unmanageable and then losing control) for anger. Instead of waiting until we get to MAX ANGER and rage, we can learn to respect our personal needs and limits, and stay attuned to ourselves well enough to recognize the subtler pointers along the way, so that we can use our emotions to inform us instead of being hijacked and controlled by them.

What Anger Really Is

Anger is an internal event. It is a spark of discomfort that tells us that something is not right and that we need to check in with ourselves to reconnect with our personal priorities, basic needs and limits. When you allow yourself to notice it, it can actually help you understand your unique priorities, needs and preferences over time.

Early Anger

Early anger can alert us to the need for care and attention and prevent future explosions if we tend to it. Resentment and critical, blaming, or judgmental feelings are all forms of early anger. It is possible to train ourselves to check in to assess our own feelings and needs when we notice feeling resentful, critical, blaming or judgmental of ourselves or others, thus heading off unmanageable stockpiles and explosions. Questions I can ask myself might look like this: Have I been tending adequately to my own basic needs? Have I been making it a habit to put others first? Is there something I need to ask for? Have I remembered to honor my own needs for:

- rest
- nutritious-enough food
- adequate exercise
- meditation/prayer at least on a fairly regular basis

If we are doing an adequate job of tending to our basic needs, it is much easier to stay grounded in the present, recognize and avoid projections, avoid making incorrect assumptions, and avoid getting triggered by situations and feelings that have the potential to send us hurtling back to childhood.

Using Early Anger to Help Connect Past to Present

In fact, early anger can serve as a bridge, helping us make the important connections between past traumas and the situations that are niggling us today. Making that connection is called "doing your emotional work" and when we can do it, it takes us that much closer to healing early relational trauma.

Doing your emotional work involves feeling the feelings, including grief. It is naming and connecting with the loss and holding it (and the young you) in your compassionate attention without distracting yourself from it, until it passes. As you learn to do this, you will feel more and more masterful about your ability to regulate your emotions instead of resorting to ego defenses and emotional dysregulation.

This is the end of Module 5, and what is intended to be the fifth week of this course. Take a few days to absorb this material. Is it time to recommit to your daily practice? Continue to gift yourself with 10-20 minutes of YOUR attention every day. Any of the activities below can be used to help you focus your attention.

Module 5 Review – Persecutor Shifts to Challenger

Online Resources:

Video: Handling the Jolting Yet Universal Truth: All Children Get Angry.
https://www.huffpost.com/entry/handling-the-jolting-yet-universal-truth-all-children_b_589ceba3e4b0e172783a9a48

Understanding the Physiological Effects of Trauma:
https://thesomaticmovement.wordpress.com/2015/07/17/red-light-means-no/

Resource to help combat urges and compulsions:
http://www.urge911.com/

Activities:

Read:
        List of things we can control (pg 122)
        Personal Bill of Rights (pg 123)
Addressing Urges and Compulsions (pg 124)
Father Work (pg 126)
What's Under Your Ego Defenses (pg 128)
Write a letter to yourself from your Inner Masculine (pg 130)
Radical Forgiveness Worksheet (pg 132)
Transforming Shoulds (pg 136)

Things You Can Control

1. Your beliefs
2. Your attitude
3. Your thoughts
4. Your perspective
5. How honest you are
6. Who your friends are
7. What books you read
8. How often you exercise
9. How many risks you take
10. What type of food you eat
11. How kind you are to others
12. How you interpret situations
13. How kind you are to yourself
14. How you express your feelings
15. How often you say "I love you."
16. How often you say "Thank you."
17. Whether or not you ask for help
18. How often you practice gratitude
19. How many times you smile today
20. The amount of effort you put forth
21. How you spend/invest your money
22. How much time you spend worrying
23. How often you identify with your past
24. Whether or not you try again after a setback
25. How much you appreciate the things you have
26. Whether or not you judge other people or yourself

Personal Bill of Rights

1. I have a right to ask for what I want.

2. I have a right to say no to requests or demands that I cannot meet.

3. I have a right to express all of my feelings—positive and negative.

4. I have a right to change my mind.

5. I have the right to go at my own pace.

6. I have a right to make mistakes and do not have to be perfect.

7. I have a right to follow my own values and beliefs.

8. I have a right to say no to anything if I feel that I am not ready.

9. I have the right to say no to anything if it is unsafe.

10. I have the right to say no to anything if it conflicts with my values.

11. I have a right to determine my own priorities.

12. I have a right not to be responsible for the actions, feelings, or behavior of others.

13. I have the right to expect honesty from others.

14. I have the right to be angry at someone I love.

15. I have the right to be myself. To be unique.

16. I have the right to express fear.

17. I have the right to say, "I don't know."

18. I have the right not to give excuses or reasons for my behavior.

19. I have the right to make decisions based on my feelings.

20. I have the right to my own personal space and time.

21. I have a right to be playful.

22. I have the right to be healthier (happier) than those around me.

23. I have the right to feel safe, and be in a nonabusive environment.

24. I have the right to make friends and be comfortable around people.

25. I have the right to change and grow.

26. I have the right to have my wants and needs respected by others.

27. I have the right to be treated with dignity and respect.

28. I have the right to be happy.

Four-Step Approach to Responding to Urges and Compulsions

1) Name the experience (just naming it helps reduce the stress).
- I am aware that I'm having a compulsion to _____.
- I'm aware that I'm having this sensation of _____.
- I'm aware that I'm having the emotion of _____ because of _____.

2) Frame the behavior and identify its function in the past.
- This makes sense because this is what my brain learned to do when I felt powerless, etc.

or
- It's just my younger scared self; she has a real need, and I am interested in identifying and tending to it.

or
- This is happening because I need:
  - a sense of relief.
  - a way to escape.
  - a way to express my voice.
  - etc.

3) Ask: How would I like this to go differently?

Example: *I see myself being able to excuse myself briefly (to check in with myself) instead of pretending that I'm engaged in a conversation (but I'm really shutting down and waiting for it to be over).*

4) Concentrate on something other than the urge (Focused Attention).

(REPEAT AS NECESSARY)

Focused attention actually re-wires the brain (when you can successfully resist the urge). This activity through which you focus your attention can be anything meaningful and productive that requires your attention.

Modified from Castlewood Treatment Center for Eating Disorders
See also www.Urge911.com

Father Work

We all have a father. Whether his role in your life was to provide the DNA for your genetic makeup or to raise and mentor you; to play with you and teach you about the world, he provides an indelible impression that impacts you and how you relate to men and the world. And whether he is known to you or not, living or not, you can still benefit from exploring your relationship with him.

Writing Exercise

1. Using a separate journal or several sheets of paper, write down any memories you have about your father from your early years. Even if they are just glimpses, or impressions.
2. What have you heard from relatives and other community members about your father? What was he like from their perspective? Does that match up with your observations and experience of him?
3. How did your father step up for you? What moved him? What were his dreams and aspirations, his values?
4. Bring an image of his face or his physical essence into your imagination and notice how your body feels.
5. Imagine the smallness of yourself when you were 4 or 5 years old, and think about his physical largeness in comparison to you. Imagine your five-year-old self in a room you would have likely inhabited with your father. How does that feel? Do you make contact? What kind? Are you touching, talking, laughing, cowering, uncomfortable, insecure?
6. If your father was active in your life, he was likely one of the people who introduced you to the world in one way or another. Write about how he acted as a bridge to the larger world, outside of the home.
7. What would you most like your father to know about you, from the perspective of your 10 year old self? Write for 10 minutes whatever comes to mind. If nothing comes to mind, how do you feel about that?
8. Visit your teenage self and bring to mind a time you were in the presence of your father. Notice the physical proximity. Notice if this feels different from before.
9. Based on how he interacted with you (or didn't), what do you think your father thought of you? In what ways did he approve of you, your behaviors, your appearance, your clothing, your mannerisms, your accomplishments, your personality?
10. What did your father do that annoyed you most?
11. What did he not do that impacted you the most?
12. What happened to your father that accounts for his deficits?
13. Were/Are you afraid of your father? Why?
14. Were/Are you worried about him? Why?

15. Were/Are you angry with him? Why?
16. What good things did you get from your father directly or indirectly?
17. What did he believe about the world? How does that compare with what you believe about the world?
18. If your father is no longer living, how has this changed how you feel about him?
19. If you could change one thing about your father, what would it be?
20. Think about the men in your life who have contributed positively, who have supported you in some way, even if from a distance. Make a list of those gifts and qualities, and feel your gratitude toward them.
21. One by one, write out a complete list of characteristics, or things that endear these people to you, or inspire you.
22. Notice how these characteristics exist, also, in you, or you are – right now – in the process of developing them.

23. Imagine an "other-worldly" father that is a conglomerate of all the positive attributes that you have experienced in the men you have known (or experienced from a distance), and let yourself enjoy how that feels. If you can conjure an image, let yourself do that to add another layer of validity to this entity so you can more easily retrieve him in the future.

24. Find a name that fits this "other-worldly father" that you like, and that feels just right. Notice where and how you feel that in your body.

25. Know that this feeling is available to you anytime you direct your energy here. It belongs to you, and nobody can take it away from you.

What's Under Your Ego Defenses?

1) What kinds of ego defenses do you use to avoid your unwanted feelings?

2) What kinds of vulnerable feelings are hidden beneath your ego defenses?

3) What unmet needs are you identifying?

4) When you identify these unmet needs, what kinds of feelings come up?

5) What stories need to be told about these feelings?

6) Is there one or more things you would be willing to do toward meeting these needs now?

From Your Inner Masculine (sample letter*):

My Dearest Beloved,

It has been a great loss that I have not been more apparent to you during the first part of your life. I therefore step up and fully assume this position now. From the moment you were born it has been clear to me how unique and beautiful you are. Take these truths now into your heart and mind. They are true, and I have no reason to deceive you.

If it is your desire, I give you permission, now, to be all you came here to be, to be a woman in all senses of the word - to experience the joy of physical mastery and pleasure. Precious one, you are the master of your experience and it is yours to explore pleasure and find what gives you joy and fulfillment. Know that this sometimes is best done by experiencing what you don't like, but it does not always have to be so.

Go ahead. Take those steps. I will be here to support you if you're not sure at first. I am here. I will continue to be here, whatever direction you decide to go, you will not disappoint me. I promise you this. Trust yourself. Your instincts are good. Your judgment, your discernment can be trusted. I am so proud of you, and excited about this work you have been doing, and what you will do next.

I love you. You deserve deep satisfaction, contentment, and the fulfilment of your heart's desires. You are good. You are pure. You are kind. You are enough.

Go forth. Be yourself.

Your Inner Masculine.

*Adapt as necessary so that gender feels appropriate, remembering that we all have both feminine and masculine aspects.

Write your own letter from your Inner Masculine

Radical Forgiveness Worksheet

When you find yourself making judgments, feeling self-righteous or wanting to change something about a situation, use this process to bring your consciousness into the present, to let go of the illusion and to align with spiritual truth.

Look at what I created!

This first step reminds us that we are the creators of our lives and that we have in fact set up all the circumstances in the situation we find ourselves upset about to help us learn and grow spiritually or heal a wound or core belief that keeps us out of our joy and bliss.

Resentment (Name of person, event, condition, experience):

1. The situation causing my discomfort, as I perceive it now, is:

2. Confronting (X): I am upset with you because:

2b. Because of what you did (are doing), I feel: (abused, abandoned, betrayed, rejected, fearful, not enough, lied to, etc.)

3. I lovingly recognize and accept my feelings and judge them no more.

    Willing   Open   Skeptical   Unwilling

4. I own my feelings. No one can make me feel anything. My feelings are a reflection of how I see the situation.

    Willing   Open   Skeptical   Unwilling

5. Even though I don't know why or how, I now see that my soul has created this situation in order that I learn and grow.

    Willing   Open   Skeptical   Unwilling

6. I am noticing some clues about my life such as repeating patterns and other features of my life that indicate that I have had many such healing opportunities in the past but I didn't recognize them as such at the time. For example:

7. I am willing to see that my mission or soul contract included having experiences like this for whatever reason.

Willing   Open   Skeptical   Unwilling

8. My discomfort was my signal that I was withholding love from myself and (X) by judging, holding expectations, wanting (X) to change and seeing (X) as less than perfect. (List the judgments, expectations and behaviors that indicate you were wanting (X) to change):

9. I now realize that I get upset only when someone resonates in me those parts of me I have disowned, denied, repressed and then projected onto them.

Willing   Open   Skeptical   Unwilling

10. (X) is reflecting what I need to love and heal in myself.

Willing   Open   Skeptical   Unwilling

11. (X) is reflecting a misperception of mine. In forgiving (X), I heal myself and recreate my reality.

Willing   Open   Skeptical   Unwilling

12. I now realize that nothing (X), or anyone else, has done is either right or wrong. I drop all judgment.

Willing   Open   Skeptical   Unwilling

13. I release the need to blame and to be right and I am WILLING to see the perfection in the situation just the way it is.

Willing   Open   Skeptical   Unwilling

14. Even though I may not know what, why, or how, I now realize that you and I have both been receiving exactly what we each had subconsciously chosen and were doing a healing dance with and for each other.

Willing   Open   Skeptical   Unwilling

15. I bless you (X) for being willing to play a part in my healing and honor myself for being willing to play a part in your healing.

Willing   Open   Skeptical   Unwilling

16. I release from my consciousness all feelings of: (as in number 2b above)

17. I appreciate your willingness, (X), to mirror my misperceptions, and I bless you for providing me with the opportunity to practice forgiveness and self-acceptance.

I now realize that what I was experiencing (my victim story) was a precise reflection of my unhealed perception of the situation. I now understand that I can change this reality by simply being willing to see the perfection in the situation. (Attempt Radical Forgiveness reframe which may simply be a general statement indicating that you just know everything is perfect, or specific to your situation if you can actually see what the gift is, i.e., the reason this person abandoned me was to show me that my abandonment issues are ready to be healed).

I completely forgive myself (your name) and accept myself as a loving, generous and creative being. I release all need to hold onto emotions and ideas of lack and limitation connected to the past. I withdraw my energy from the past and release all barriers against the love and abundance that I know I have in this moment. I create my life and I am empowered to be myself again, to unconditionally love and support myself, just the way I am, in all my power and magnificence.

I now surrender to my higher power I think of as _____ and trust in the knowledge that this situation will continue to unfold perfectly and in accordance with Divine guidance and spiritual law. I acknowledge my Oneness and feel myself totally reconnected with my source. I am restored to my true nature, which is LOVE, and I now restore love to _____.

Having done this work, I, _____, completely forgive you, _____, for I now realize that you did nothing wrong and that everything is in Divine order. I acknowledge, accept and love you unconditionally just the way you are.

To myself: I recognize that I am a spiritual being having a human experience, and I love and support myself in every aspect of my humanness.

This is an exercise that comes from the book, *Radical Forgiveness* by Colin Tipping. Reading the book and doing the exercises in it are an excellent way to focus your attention and take advantage of the exaggerated feelings during an emotional flashback! Used with permission.

Transforming Shoulds

Shoulds signal that we are afraid. They are a collection of hard-to-verbalize feelings, but if we can get them down in writing, we can begin to transform them into feelings and needs. What follows is how it looks to transform shoulds into feelings and needs.

Outer Shoulds	Taking responsibility for our feelings and needs looks like this:
• People shouldn't make "incorrect" assumptions.	When people make assumptions, I feel angry, because I need respect.
• People should get my permission before entering my house or touching my things.	When people enter my house without permission I feel startled, alarmed and defensive because I need safety and dependability.
• People shouldn't touch or take my things without my permission or some kind of prior understanding.	When people touch or take my things I feel violated and defensive. I need gentleness, respect, and consideration.

See if you can capture the shoulds that have been lurking in your mind. If you can catch them, they will help you identify feelings and needs.

Inner Shoulds	Taking responsibility for feelings and needs:

Inner Shoulds	Taking responsibility for feelings and needs:

Module 5 Quiz 1:

1) What are good signs that our inner environment has become hostile (that we have reverted to defenses instead of a conscious, fully empowered response)?
   A. Blaming
   B. Shaming
   C. Criticizing
   D. Ridiculing
   E. Complaining
   F. All of the above
   G. A-D above

2) Which of the following are examples of focused attention activities that could be used to rewire the brain?

   A. Journaling
   B. Winning an argument with my neighbor
   C. Worrying
   D. Gardening
   E. All of the above
   F. A & D above

3) Which of the following statements would Challenger never say?

   A. Knowledge is power.
   B. Urges and compulsions are things that our BRAIN learned how to do as a once-adaptive response to stress.
   C. Focused attention re-wires the brain.
   D. No pain, no gain.
   E. There are things you have control over, and other things that you don't.

4) (True or False) Shaming is a form of manipulation and abuse.

5) The following is not a sign of Early Anger
   A. Resentment
   B. Critical feelings
   C. Impulse to blame
   D. Judgmental feelings
   E. Blowing up in response to a joke that strikes me the wrong way.

Module 6 - The Sacred Marriage

The function of parents is to raise children to be healthy, capable, socially adept adults. It is their job to ensure safety, and foster an environment in which the child can explore who they are so they can grow and mature to their full potential. For people who grew up in the presence of the Drama Triangle, feeling safe in the body or being attuned to the body's full range of sensory and sensual capability never even made it onto the syllabus. And "feeling safe" was, frankly, just words.

What if People Felt Safe?

What would the range of human behavior be if people were safe? This is a question that has sparked the curiosity of research scientist and Professor Stephen Porges, PhD. "The potential of the individual and humanity will really only occur in the context of safety," his message goes. Porges is the author of "The Polyvagal Theory," which explains the physiology behind social engagement, and why some people can be calmed by the presence of another, while others clearly cannot. At the end of this module I include a link where you can watch an interview with Porges at Dharma Café.

The issue of *felt* safety is what is being explored in the attachment literature today, and as it turns out, feeling safe is not just something that happens in the mind, but is something that imprints on the body, affecting how we carry ourselves through life, how we relate with others, and to what extent we reach for what we want in life. As we heard from Stuart Brown, it isn't possible to lose ourselves in play if we don't feel safe. So for children who learn to shut down, disconnect, defend and pretend, important development opportunities are lost.

Porges has gained considerable attention for his work with a particular part of the nervous system only present in humans and higher mammals (the myelinated vagus), that is directly responsible for allowing the body to relax in the presence of another. Porges explains in the video how the engagement of the myelinated vagus is a biological symbol that one's nervous system is safe.

The engaged myelinated vagus allows for higher mammals to experience:

> *Positive affective experience*
> *Social engagement behavior*
> *Relationship building*
> *Opportunities for spirituality*

This is basically a list of the things that people miss out on when their nervous systems are chronically defensive. As adults, what we stand to gain when we learn how to engage the myelinated vagus are vastly increased capacity for peace, compassion, contentment and happiness, spontaneous and authentic self-expression, and a readily accessible felt sense that we will be okay regardless of what happens.

Focused Attention and Play

There is a switch inside of each one of us that we can learn to operate by understanding the body. And how we manage our internal environment has a huge impact on our bodies. When we engage gratitude and curiosity, we cannot simultaneously remain hyper-aroused, critical or terrified. Likewise, judgmental, evaluative, and defensive thoughts are neurophysiologically incompatible with feelings of confidence and compassion. That is just how our nervous systems work. Focused attention is one of the few magic bullets that consistently flips that switch in the body to move us to a place of safety and calmness.

Porges believes that we can consciously engage the myelinated vagus through safe forms of play, and focused attention is a very close parallel to play. When was the last time you watched a child fully absorbed in his or her own version of creative play? Imagine it now. They are absorbed in the task with an energized focus. Defenses and need for control are turned off. They are in flow. Nothing else exists. Children naturally play unless they are trained not to. The critical work of retraining is ours to do.

Make some kind of focused attention activity a regular part of your daily routine. Since self-care routines are often the first thing to go in times of high stress, be proactive. Select 6-12 focused attention activities that best suit your learning style and needs. Print them out or write them down and keep them in a place you can easily find them when you need them. Focused attention activities, whether in the form of walking meditation, journaling, creative play, chanting, breath work, tai chi or some kind of mental device, will give you the foundation you need as you work toward calming your nervous system, rewiring your brain, and internalizing your own loving and safe inner parents.

Depending on your unique history, learning style, and needs, flipping the switch might require an activity that is more physical or more mental. Or you could need something more interpersonal. The key is that the activity is focused, and appealing enough to fully engage you in the face of an urge or compulsion. Most importantly, focused attention can be used to discharge the energy of the old repressed emotions and flip the switch in the body so that it can relax once more.

The Body Temple

The relaxed body is a magnificent temple that is designed to interface flawlessly with Creator. When we adopt the habit and skills of allowing Creator to have a voice in our system, we begin to move with more flow, instinct and grace. With Creator's innocent unselfconsciousness, honesty and capacity for play we can be nimble, receptive and responsive in the moment. We can deal appropriately in each situation that we encounter, even if it is not what we expected or reminds us of something from the past. Having and consistently using the skills and tools of Coach and Challenger helps Creator feel safe and the body to relax.

As it turns out, the connection between the central nervous system and social relationships is bidirectional. If we can learn to calm the body enough, we can more readily benefit from the physical presence of other calm and loving people. And the more we can surround ourselves with calm and loving people, the more calm our nervous systems will become.

Becoming good stewards of the body temple involves just as much unlearning as it does learning. Living in a relaxed body makes a tremendous difference in how we interact with other people and the world. This week, let's gently shift to body-focused exercises and activities. These are ways to focus attention too. But they are specifically designed to support a more safe and conscious dialogue with the body. With the help of a short recording or script, you can focus your attention while exploring your relationship with your body, and while doing so, up-level your mastery in the realm of your "felt sense." When you can do that, you can learn to slowly relax muscles that you have unconsciously held tense, and begin to live in a body that tells your brain and the people around you that you are grounded in the here and now and not protecting yourself from some unseen, unremembered threat. At the end of this module I include a list of simple body-focused activities you can try.

Asking for What We Want and Need

Another critical thing that good parenting provides is an environment where the child is invited to explore who she is and what she wants. It takes the support of calm and attentive parents to help the child know that his or her desires are actually very important navigational tools, and that they should be used. All is not lost if your home was chaotic and your parents distracted or stressed, however, because experiencing things you don't like really does help you get clear on what you would like instead. It's just one short step away from claiming what you want and need without guilt or shame.

Chances are, since childhood you have experienced a great many beautiful, positive things. Just like the trauma and stress you have experienced during your lifetime, this information collects in your memory, and it is available for you to draw upon. Spending time identifying and naming those positive things is a very powerful way to cultivate crucial self-knowledge and help you get clear on what you would like more of. "Resource Memories" might include places in nature, cherished animals, cherished people who appeared for a brief time in your life, moments where you felt like yourself – powerful or grounded, things that you have accomplished and done well, or even characters and scenes from books and movies.

Some of the focused attention activities in this course may have helped you get clearer on what you want more of. You may be able to look back over your journals and transform those things you have not enjoyed into knowledge about what you actually want. Think back over the activities you have done so far and collect the precious bits you have gleaned from them. Constructing a life that suits you well is something that starts in your imagination, when you finally feel yourself to be worthy.

Finally, once recognizing your wants, needs and desires becomes more familiar to you, it will become more natural to take that next step and claim them for yourself.

The Secure Base

As Porges says, we can produce bold new knowledge if we feel the connection and support of a secure base. This secure base is completely within our reach as adults. By now you should be familiar with the cast of characters and features of the Empowerment Triangle and the Sacred Marriage and have a growing sense of a reliable secure base, from which you can venture out and risk new experiences and new levels of authenticity, spontaneity and confidence. The following formula captures the core message of this course in a format that is readily accessible when you need it to help you remember how to give yourself the compassionate attention you need and deserve. As your confidence and mastery take root and grow, you will experience firsthand the deliciousness of safety, and this way of being with yourself will become automatic and internalized.

The Formula for Internalizing a Secure Base

Throughout this course I've referred to the "gentle shift" and the "slight pivot" of Rescuer to Coach and Persecutor to Challenger. I choose these words hoping to convey that this transition is best done not through excising or blotting out or amputating parts of ourselves, but by re-directing our life-preserving instincts. Then, rather than merely keeping us alive and helping us cope, this energy can be what we use to step into our creative genius, utilizing the authenticity of our supported, fully-embodied selves.

As you redouble your commitment to doing what is necessary to live in the here and now, calm in body and mind, at peace with yourself, responding to the information that is available to you through your senses, any unkindness you may direct at yourself will more easily and automatically be redirected to grounded, embodied presence. The following framework outlines the steps you might adopt as a formula for internalizing your own loving, safe parents.

Pause (Three Deep Breaths)
Check-In Approach
Coach/Inner Feminine
Challenger/Inner Masculine

Creator/TVP
Pause (Body Scan)
How would I like this to go differently in the future?

The Dance

Inner Masculine defers to Inner Feminine when it comes to emotions, compassion and attunement. Inner Masculine provides structure and safety and just enough distance from the intensity of the past. They share information so that Inner Feminine can benefit from the work that Inner Masculine does, and Inner Masculine can be informed by the work that Inner Feminine does. Good parenting can't happen without the skills and abilities of both. Don't worry about getting it exactly right. You are allowed to learn as you go. Don't worry about "spoiling" your inner child. Creator is a reliable source of information, keeping you anchored in what suits you, what delights you, and what you want and need. It is wise to listen to it. Stay attuned to your tender, vulnerable parts to inform your decisions, large and small, and add confidence, joy and playfulness to your life.

Make sure to watch the powerful 3-minute video included in the review where Oprah Winfrey embodies the wisdom of the integrated Sacred Marriage.

The Dance

1) (Pause) Three Deep Breaths

2) Check-In

Coach
- Offers compassion.
- Notices the emotion or early emotion.
  - ✓ You have survived a great storm. You are safe now.
  - ✓ You did the best you could.
  - ✓ What have you been afraid to ask for?
  - ✓ What do you need in order to feel safe?
  - ✓ What adjustments need to be made so that it is actually safe to be completely present right now?
  - ✓ What support is needed to help you feel safe enough to want what you want and know what you know?
  - ✓ What are you feeling now?
  - ✓ What are you needing now?
  - ✓ What was all that complaining about?
  - ✓ What would you really like?

143

Challenger
- Provides safety and structure
  - ✓ What is your intention in this situation?
  - ✓ What needs to happen in order for you to take charge of your life?
    - ✓ Allies with Coach
    - ✓ Recognizes the ingenuity of the old strategies and appreciates your creative, resilient mind.
    - ✓ How can you discharge the energy of this emotion without beating up on yourself or hurting someone else?
    - ✓ Supports accountability, growth and next steps
    - ✓ What have you learned from situations like this in the past?
    - ✓ What real and valuable skills have you gained as a result of this difficult path?
    - ✓ What are the obvious life-affirming solutions you have been resisting?

Creator
- Tells you about your feelings and needs via the body.
  - ✓ PLAY (Shift attention to something other than the urge – engage in Focused Attention – for 10-20 minutes).

3) (Pause) Body Scan
4) How would you like this to go differently in the future?

(REPEAT AS NECESSARY)

This is the end of Module 6, and what is intended to be the sixth week of this course. This does not mean that you are done taking care of yourself. This week, continue to focus attention, but with special emphasis on your body. Remember that your body is your sacred temple, and it holds vast stores of wisdom, guidance and pleasure.

Module 6 Review – The Sacred Marriage

Videos:

Stephen Porges – "The Polyagal Theory" https://www.youtube.com/watch?v=8tz146HQotY

 There Are No Mistakes – Oprah Winfrey https://www.youtube.com/watch?v=dGgb1PwH7mo

Activities:

Rite of Passage - Adolescence Exercise (pg 146)

Gratitude as a Mental Exercise (pg 148)

Capturing the Voices of Your Internal Parts (pg 150)

Manifesting (pg 152)

Visioning (pg 154)

Application:

Body Scan Master List (pg 156)

Check-In Approach for Responding to Urges and Compulsions (pg 176)

Case Example (pg 178)

Rite of Passage - Adolescence

The following exercise ideas are designed to help you revisit your adolescence in a new way. Adolescence is a time of profound change, not only in terms of responsibility and physical maturity, but also in terms of identity and societal expectations. The main developmental task of adolescence is individuating from parental influence - to begin to form a unique set of values that is not identical to what he or she has been taught. Use a journal or loose paper to write out your thoughts. Write until you have answered the questions, and then keep writing until you have fully expressed yourself. Chances are, your adolescent self was not listened to as much as he or she wanted or needed to be. You can change that now.

1. Think about your adolescence in relation to your mother. How did your relationship change? As you began to look more like an adult and less like a child, did she see this and feel excited and proud? Or did this seem to mark a time of less closeness, more conflict? What did your growing up mean to her?

2. Think about your adolescence in relation to your father. How did your relationship change? As you began to look more like an adult and less like a child, what happened to your relationship with your father? Did he acknowledge you as a person, or as an extension of himself? What did your growing up mean to him?

3. When did you first start noticing that your parents made mistakes, that they were just imperfect humans? Write about a few of the mistakes your parents made and notice any feelings that come up when you tell these stories. See if you can name the feelings, whether they are of the emotional variety, or if they are physical sensations in your body or your energy field.

4. Write about some of the worst mistakes you made as a teenager, and then about how your parents responded. This is not a time to see things from their perspective, but from yours. Describe what happened to the best of your ability. See if you can name your feelings fully and completely. Stand by your adolescent self while he or she pours this story out onto the page. Let yourself say what you couldn't have when you were a teenager. This time and space is just for you. It's about time you had a place just for this purpose.

5. What are the things you would not want to change about the way you were raised?

6. Write about any mentors or role models you had during your adolescent years. What roles did they play and how did they change the trajectory of your life?

7. Write briefly or in depth about your own sexual history. Document landmarks with regard to physical development and the people in your life at that time. Remember your first crush, your first boyfriend or girlfriend. Remember body sensations and write about them. What do you like to remember about this time? What would you rather forget? What do you remember about your body? Your tender unguarded self? Your mind?

8. Make a list of the feminine aspects of yourself – the sensitive, empathic, warm, receptive, intuitive side of you. Can you see her? Feel her essence? Does she have a name? Thank her for showing up.

9. Make a list of the masculine aspects of yourself – the active, analytical, outgoing, physical, get-things-done, practical side. Can you see him? Feel his essence? Does he have a name? Thank him for showing up.

10. Imagine how these two aspects of yourself might interact with one another. Explore how their roles work together to support your growth, your development, and the ease in which you can step gracefully and confidently into adulthood and your fullest potential.

Gratitude as a Mental Exercise

Since it takes five times as much energy to remember positive things as it does to remember negative things, it is important to consciously adopt habits that help us exercise our mental muscles, and that means gratitude exercises. You can do this in any way that works for you. Science shows that whether or not you actually identify things to be grateful for, the activity of searching for positive things in your mind stimulates feel-good hormones and serves as a way to focus your attention.

Flex your brain muscle in order to identify, name and embrace all that you actually appreciate in your life; the things that are going well enough or right. This is a muscle, and strengthening it takes discipline, but it's worth every minute of it. Take time every day to put your attention there. Here are a few ideas to get you started:

- List the good things that happened today.
- Review the day, focusing on what you liked.
- Think about the things you are looking forward to tomorrow, this week, or this year.
- Notice how you feel as you bring cherished things to mind, whether they are actual things or places or people in your memory or imagination.
- Use each letter of the alphabet to help you think of things that you appreciate.
- Appreciate the plants for producing oxygen and absorbing carbon dioxide.
- Appreciate your eyes, your fingers and your arms.

Capturing the Voices of Your Internal Parts

The ego is a head trip, groups of words that form themselves into repetitive patterns that chatter continuously like crickets in our mind.

-Gabrielle Roth

We all contain multitudes. Great thinkers like Freud, Carl Jung, Walt Whitman, Alfred Adler, Richard Schwartz, have long recognized this.

In this exercise, pay close attention to the various aspects of your inner self. Notice how they are in conflict, allied or at odds with each other. How they protect, rescue or war with each other. With each one in turn, tune in so that you can better hear their frequency, as if they are their own radio station. Invite them to speak clearly so that you really know them. Their needs, their fears, their experience of the world.

Feel into their essence. When did they first appear, and for what reason?

Can you see them? Could you draw or paint them? Write about how they appear, any physical attributes, how old they seem. What their favorite expressions are, their general attitudes. Get curious about what they are doing. How does each of them serve you? What greater purpose do they serve? What do they like and dislike?

See if you can capture the voice and tone of your internal parts in the space below, and then continue in your journal if you like. Write without censoring or editing your work for 10-20 minutes.

Manifesting

Materials:
- Old magazines
- Scissors
- Small box
- Paper
- Pen

Procedure: Find some old magazines and flip through the pages.   Notice textures and colors and let your eyes linger on the ones that feel pleasing to you.   Find pictures that you would like to look at some more, or that represent things you want.   Cut out the pictures that you like and collect them in the box.

On the outside of the box, write, *"Whatever is contained in this box IS."*

For each picture that you collected in the box, write on a slip of paper what it represents that you would like more of in your life.   What you are writing on each slip of paper is a thing, a condition, or an experience you want to have in your life.   Be as specific as you can when you write what you want.   The more details the better.   Continue to add slips of paper as you think of things, conditions or experiences that you want to have.

Read through the slips of paper and look at the pictures you have collected two or three times a week and let yourself anticipate what it will feel like when these things are a real part of your life.   Thank your box and your inner Creator for helping you to get clearer about what you want more of in your life.

Visioning

This is a practice that I have been using for many years. It was inspired by Shakti Gawain in her book, *Creative Visualization*, but it has evolved as I've used it over the years. Start with the list of categories below to describe the things and conditions you desire in your life. Modify it so that it suits you and your life. Don't hesitate to write down what you already like about the way things are going. But allow yourself to take sweeping liberties, embellish, and stretch your imagination, reaching for what you would really like – what would make your life even better. Keep your visioning statement in a place where you can find it later and update it as you accomplish what you set out to do and notice changes in what you are desiring. You can also make a list of 10 things that you want (but don't know how you could ever afford). Be extravagant, and see what happens. It's okay to want more!

I surrender to my soul's deepest intent
for this lifetime.
I Am Joy-Filled and Grateful!

These are the details of my desired life:

Work
Professional Growth
Finances
Relationships
Healthy Adult Intimacy
Creative Life
Co-workers
Growth
Body
Recreation
Home
Rhythms
Community
Spiritual

I thank you Spirit; I thank you Angels, and so it is!
This or something better now manifests
for the highest good of all concerned.

Body Scan Master List

Affectionate Breathing (pg 157)
Body Exposure Imagery (pg 158)
Body Gratitude Imagery (pg 160)
Felt-Sense Somatic Experiencing Exercise (pg 162)
Guided Deep Relaxation with Sister Chan Khong (pg 164)
Letter to and From Body (pg 166)
Letter to Younger Self (pg 168)
Mirror Work with a Nonjudgmental Body Scan (pg 170)
Mirror Work with Gratitude Body Scan (pg 172)
Self-Compassion Body Scan Meditation (pg 174)

Adapted From: *Body Embrace* at Alsana, An Eating Recovery Community. Compiled by Nicole Siegfried, PhD, CEDS & Amber Parris, LICSW, CEDS   nicole.siegfried@alsana.com

Affectionate Breathing (Neff, 2014)

Objective: The work of self-compassion can begin with breath work. The word "breath" can be traced to the Latin root of "Spiro," which means soul. Learning to breathe in kindness and affection can be an initial method to cultivate compassion and nourish the soul.

Instructions: A guided imagery by Kristin Neff can be found at the following site. Listen to this guided imagery. If it moves you, try listening to it once a day for a week.

http://self-compassion.org/wp-content/uploads/2016/11/affectionatebreathing_cleaned.mp3

Body Exposure Imagery

Objective: By imagining yourself in front of a mirror and scanning through the body, one can use imagery exposure as a stepping stone to body acceptance.

Instructions: You might want to simply read through the following, or you might want to print off this page and have someone read it to you, or you can make a tape of yourself reading the words. You can do a relaxation first, or not. You might want to have a journal ready to write down what you feel as you finish the meditation. If you feel like you need to stop at any time, please do so. You may experience powerful feelings from doing meditation, or no feelings, or anything in between. If you have painful emotions emerge, please treat yourself gently. Doing an exercise that puts you in touch with your body may put you in touch with emotions you have "lived above the chin" to avoid. Treat yourself with compassion. You might like some comforting - a hug or a soothing bath or a talk with a trusted friend. Consider writing down what you are feeling.

In your mind's eye, imagine yourself standing in front of a mirror where you can see most of your body. Let your eyes come to a rest upon your own eyes. Take three deep, slow breaths. As you pull the air gently into your body, and as you gently push the air out, notice the black of your pupils, and the colors that's around them, the curve of those colors. And breathe.

Take a moment to broaden your awareness to the whole of your face. Notice the frame of your face. Your hairline around to your jaw. Let yourself notice the details of your face feelings. Notice the curves of your forehead, your cheeks, your chin, your nose, and your eyebrows. Notice the hollows that's around them. And finally let your attention come to rest on the peaks of your lips and nestle there between your nose and your chin. And breathe.

And on your next breath, guide your attention down your neck and out into your shoulders. Notice the slopes that connect your arms to the rest of your body. And breathe.

Now gently let your attention flow down your arms, noticing the lines and curves that make up your arms, flesh around bone. Let your fingers spread wide as you notice each individual finger before guiding your attention back to your arms and back around your shoulders. And breathe.

Take a moment to notice the movement in your chest and belly as you breathe. Watch them rise and fall as your breath rises and falls. Bring your attention back to your hands and notice each individual finger before guiding your attention back up your arms and around your shoulders. And breathe.

Take a moment to notice the movement in your chest and belly as you breathe. Watch them rise and fall as your breath flows in and out. Let your attention trace the sides of your body, noting your edges, the places where you stop. And breathe.

And on your next breath, wrap your awareness gently along your hips, around your bottom, under and back around. And breathe and gently, gently guide your attention along your thighs from the inside around the front and the sides of your thighs. And breathe --and as you breathe, gently let your attention come to rest on your knees. Notice the way they interrupt your legs, transitioning from thighs to shin. And breathe.

Take a moment now to let your awareness flow down your leg along the shinbone. Let yourself notice your calf muscle spreading behind the bone, the curve it brings to your leg. And breathe. Now gently shift your attention into your ankles. See if you can't trace the bands that protrude to allow your ankles to bend and twist. And breathe.

Let your attention drift along the tops of your feet and take a moment now to shift your attention into your toes, one by one, from the smallest to the largest, out. And breathe.

With your final three breaths, let your eyes come to rest again on your eyes, but this time, see if you can't expand your awareness out to take in the whole of your visual experience of yourself right now. From the very tips of your toes to the very top of your head, take a moment to be still and see yourself. Let your eyes come to rest again on your eyes, but this time, see if you can't expand your awareness out to take in the whole of your visual experience of yourself right now. From the very tips of your toes to the very top of your head, take a moment to be still and see yourself.

Body Gratitude Imagery (adapted from Sobczack & Scott, 2017)

Objective: Utilizing imagery to create gratitude can foster acceptance in a more powerful way because it integrates more of an experiential event.

Instructions: So much of the time we are either taking our bodies for granted or actively disparaging them. And yet they keep serving us, day after day. Take a few moments to think about how your body has been loyally functioning on your behalf. There is no "right" way to reflect. You might want to simply read through the following, or you might want to copy this page and have someone read it to you, or you can make a recording of yourself reading the words. You can do a relaxation first, or not. You might want to have a journal ready to write down what you feel as you finish the meditation. If you feel like you need to stop at any time, please do so. You may experience powerful feelings from doing meditation, or no feelings, or anything in between. If you have painful emotions emerge, please treat yourself gently. Doing an exercise that puts you in touch with your body may put you in touch with emotions you have "lived above the chin" to avoid. Treat yourself with compassion. You might like some comforting - a hug or a soothing bath or a talk with a trusted friend. Consider writing down what you are feeling.

Close your eyes and let your awareness settle gradually on your breath, traveling in and out. You do not need to try to breathe, your breath just breathes itself effortlessly. Allow yourself to feel the support of the cushions beneath you and behind you, the floor beneath your feet. Notice any sensations in your body: places where you may feel an itch, or an ache, chill or warmth, or an emptiness, or a fullness . . . or even places that seem to feel numb. Just sit with this awareness of your body for a moment.

Imagine the path of your breath, traveling into and out of your body. As it comes in it warms your body, flowing through your nose, down your throat, into your lungs. You can imagine that it keeps flowing down, warming your stomach, your pelvis, radiating out into your limbs, all the way to the tips of your fingers and toes. Your breath travels through your body, and as you breathe out, you take any tension that it finds out of your body. Like a warm ocean wave, your breath brings in relaxation, and takes away tension. Feel these waves for a few moments.

Now listen to all the ways that you may have experienced a gift from your body lately. As you listen, let your mind create pictures of the recent past, pictures that fade in and out, creating a kaleidoscope of images.

Perhaps your body has:
- ✓ Fought off an infection
- ✓ Taken you to the top of a hill
- ✓ Stayed awake so you could drive home safely
- ✓ Learned a new physical skill
- ✓ Rewarded you with the sight of a sunset
- ✓ Healed a bruise

- ✓ Given you a new sensual sensation
- ✓ Gotten stronger
- ✓ Kept working despite being in pain
- ✓ Expressed a strong emotion through your face or body language
- ✓ Created another human being
- ✓ Defended you from an attack, or healed from an attack
- ✓ Grown into its current form from two cells: a sperm and an egg
- ✓ Given you sexual pleasure
- ✓ Let you know through pain that something needs your attention
- ✓ Released you from pain
- ✓ Given you the sound of children laughing
- ✓ Rejuvenated during sleep
- ✓ Allowed you to feel the exquisite touch of another person

Notice any feelings you are having as you let these images come and go. Perhaps you are feeling some positive feelings toward your body, and perhaps there are also some angry or frustrated feelings too. Let all of your feelings be present and just notice them.

Think of one thing in particular that you appreciate. It may be hard, but try to let a focus happen.

Let yourself feel the specialness of this gift from your body, the awe and wonder of it. What would you like to say to your body from this place of appreciation? Create a phrase that expresses your appreciation. Take some time to let this phrase form in your mind.

Now say your phrase to your body self. Notice how you feel saying it, and how you feel hearing it. Maybe this is something you could make time to say more often.

Think of a time during your day when you want to be aware of this body appreciation. It could be any time of your day, but pick a situation that usually happens as a matter of your daily routine already. Whatever this time and place is, it only needs to allow you a few moments of reflection.

What is happening at this time of day? Visualize the environment in as much detail as possible - sights, sounds, smells, sensations of touch, temperature, texture, etc. Now visualize yourself saying your body appreciation phrase. Imagine yourself having feelings about saying it, and hearing yourself say it.

Resolve to let this situation trigger the thought of your body appreciation phrase so that you can feel this appreciation for your body, sincerely and deeply, every day.

Notice any thoughts or feelings you are having before you allow your awareness to return to your surroundings. Now you may want to write about the feelings that came up for you during the meditation. Remember, you may have had powerful feelings or no feelings, or anything in between. There is no "right" set of feelings or images. Try to encourage an attitude of curiosity and respect for whatever your experience is.

Felt-Sense Somatic Experiencing Exercise (Levine, 2010)

Objective: Develop the ability to be in tune with and describe your "felt sense" (the sensations occurring on subtle and overt levels in all areas of the body) with the help of a safe guide.

Instructions: Before beginning this exercise, read the list, *Qualities of the Felt Sense* below. Ask a trusted person to guide you through this exercise while you sit or lie down in a quiet location where you can comfortably focus. You will need your guide to ask you to describe the sensations you notice in your body.

Guide's Script: Pay attention to the more subtle sensations in your body and use as many descriptive words as possible. I will guide you to put your attention on different parts of your body to help you notice what you are feeling there.

Wrists	Feet
Hands	Hair
Chest	Skin
Waist	Eyes
Stomach	Nose
Hips	Mouth
Buttocks	Teeth
Thighs	Chin
Calves	Neck
Ankles	Shoulders
	Upper arms

Guide: Use your intuition to guide your friend. This should be light, slow (long pauses are good), gentle and explorative, and last for 10 – 15 minutes. You may try picking a handful of body parts, say 5, and ask either/or questions using the list below for ideas. For example, *Does it feel more rough or more smooth? Is it slow or fast? Does it feel heavy or light?*

To finish, guide your friend to relax and notice the breath for 2 – 3 more minutes before gently rolling onto the side, and pushing up. Invite your friend to share their experience, and then trade roles.

Examples of Qualities of the Felt Sense:

1) feeling/sensation
    a. pressure – even, uneven, supportive feeling, crushed feeling, cutting off circulation
    b. air current – gentle, cool, warm, from right/left, stimulating, rush, like a feather, like mist
    c. tension – solid, dense, warm, cold, inflamed, protective, constricting, angry, sad
    d. pain – ache, sharp, twinge, slight, stabbing

e. tingling – pricks, vibration, tickling, numb

f. itch – mild itch, angry itch, irritating itch, moving itch, subtle itch, small/large itch

2) temperature – warm, hot, burning, cool, cold, clammy, chills, icy, frozen, like: hearth, oven, fire, sunshine, baked bread, snow, stone, shade

3) size – small, large

4) shape – flat, circle, blob, like a mountain

5) weight – light, heavy

6) motion – circular, erratic, straight line

7) speed – fast, slow, still

8) texture – rough, wood, stone, sandpaper, smooth, silk

9) element – fire, air, earth, water, wood

10) color – gray, blue, orange etc.

11) mood/emotion – sinking, pulling in, open, closed, uplifting, sunny day, dark cloud, roiling

12) sound – buzzing, singing

13) taste – sour, bitter, sweet

14) smell – pungent, sweet, like rain, like leaves

15) absence/nothingness – blank, empty

Guided Deep Relaxation with Sister Chan Khong

Objective: Directing our compassionate attention to the body.

Instructions: A guided imagery by Sister Chan Khong can be found at the following site. Listen to this guided imagery at least once a day.

https://soundcloud.com/tamthiencan/guided-deep-relaxation-with

Letter to and From Body

Objective: Renewing or establishing a loving relationship between yourself and your body.

Instructions: Write a letter of compassion toward your body. Write a similar letter from your body to yourself.

Letter to Younger Self

Objective: Self-compassion can be a difficult emotion to cultivate. Sometimes it is easier to begin the practice of compassion by working with a younger version of ourselves. If this is still too threatening, you can work on creating compassion for a "young girl" or a "young boy."

Instructions: Write a letter of compassion to a younger version of yourself at the age you were when you began developing negative body image. What would you want to say to that young person? As you're writing this letter, non-compassionate feelings may arise. That's ok. Either allow these thoughts to pass by and come back to a place of compassion or write these non-compassionate thoughts down to come back to at a later time.

Mirror Work with a Nonjudgmental Body Scan (Delinsky et al.)

Objective: Provide neutral comments on 20 different body parts (i.e., hair, skin, eyes, nose, mouth, teeth, chin, neck, shoulders, upper arms, wrists, hands, chest, waist, hips, buttocks, thighs, calves, ankles, and feet), while observing your body in a full length mirror. Post a list of these body parts on the edge of the mirror to guide you during the exposure.

Instructions: There is no wrong way to do this exercise. You can do a relaxation first, or not. You might want to have a journal ready to write down what you feel as you finish the exercise. If you feel like you need to stop at any time, please do so. You may experience powerful feelings from doing the exercise, or no feelings, or anything in between. If painful emotions emerge, please treat yourself gently. Doing an exercise that puts you in touch with your body may put you in touch with emotions you have "lived above the chin" to avoid. Treat yourself with compassion. You might like some comforting - a hug or a soothing bath or a talk with a trusted friend. Consider writing down what you are feeling.

Guidelines: Describe your body parts, out loud, from head to toe. It is important that you do not skip over OR dwell on any parts, but rather, give equal attention to everything you see. Also, do not use critical or unkind language, such as "fat," "too big," "gross," or "flabby." Instead, use objective, nonjudgmental descriptors, such as those relating to color, texture, proportion, shape, or symmetry. This is kind of like describing yourself to someone who is drawing you, but cannot see you. This exercise may seem difficult, but try your best to stick with it until you have described each body part.

Wrists	Feet
Hands	Hair
Chest	Skin
Waist	Eyes
Stomach	Nose
Hips	Mouth
Buttocks	Teeth
Thighs	Chin
Calves	Neck
Ankles	Shoulders
	Upper arms

Mirror Work with Gratitude Body Scan

Instructions: Do this exercise for about 10 minutes. Make a commitment to doing it for several days in a row. If you feel like you need to stop, give yourself permission to do so. You may experience powerful feelings, or no feelings, or anything in between. Doing an exercise that puts you in touch with your body may also put you in touch with emotions you have made it a habit to avoid. Treat yourself with compassion. Consider keeping a journal on what you experience over the days you do the exercise.

Stand in front of a mirror in the least amount of clothing you feel comfortable. In this exercise you will scan through your body parts in the mirror and state at least one thing that makes you grateful for that body part. For example, you might say, "I love my arms because they are muscular and strong." If this is too difficult, it might be helpful to begin with making amends for the way you have treated your body.

For instance, you may say, "I want to say I'm sorry to my thighs for saying that you were fat and gross and I want to have a better relationship with you." Consider making amends with body parts the way you would with another cherished individual.

You may notice negative thoughts creeping into your practice. If this happens, it's ok. Just allow those thoughts to drift naturally out and continue to focus on carrying out the task at hand.

When coming back to the exercise on subsequent days, begin with the same body parts that you used on the previous day, stating something loving, compassionate, or apologetic, and then moving on to other body parts as you are ready.

Self-Compassion Body Scan Meditation (Albertson, Neff, & Dill-Shakleford, 2014)

Objective: This exercise is designed to help a person get in touch with body sensations and bring a sense of compassion and peace to his/her body.

Instructions: A guided imagery of this exercise by Kristin Neff can be found at the following site. Clients are instructed to listen to this once a day.

http://self-compassion.org/wp-content/uploads/2016/11/bodyscan_cleaned.mp3

Check-In Approach
for Responding to Urges and Compulsions

1. (Pause) Three Deep Breaths

2. Check-In

Coach
- *Notices the emotion or early emotion.*
- *Offers compassion.*
    - ✓ *You have survived a great storm. You are safe now.*
    - ✓ *You did the best you could.*
    - ✓ *What have you been afraid to ask for?*
    - ✓ *What do you need in order to feel safe?*
    - ✓ *What adjustments need to be made so that it is actually safe to be completely present right now?*
    - ✓ *What support is needed to help you feel safe enough to want what you want and know what you know?*
    - ✓ *What are you feeling now?*
    - ✓ *What are you needing now?*
    - ✓ *What was all that complaining about?*
    - ✓ *What would you really like?*

Challenger
- *Provides safety and structure*
    - ✓ *What is your intention in this situation?*
    - ✓ *What needs to happen in order for you to take charge of your life?*
- *Allies with Coach*
    - ✓ *Recognizes the ingenuity of the old strategies and appreciates your creative, resilient mind.*
    - ✓ *How can you discharge the energy of this emotion without beating up on yourself or hurting someone else?*
- *Supports accountability, growth and next steps*

✓ *What have you learned from situations like this in the past?*

✓ *What real and valuable skills have you gained as a result of this difficult path?*

✓ *What are the obvious life-affirming solutions you have been resisting?*

Creator

- *Tells me about my feelings and needs*
- *Shift focus to something other than the urge (Focused Attention) for 10-20 minutes.*

3) (Pause) Body Scan

4) How would I like this to go differently in the future?

Case Example

Client Trying to Establish an Adequate Support Team (history of experiencing prolonged emotional flashbacks): *I am worried that there is something I am doing that is sabotaging any attempt at getting real support from a psychotherapist, and that until I figure out what that is, I will just be wasting time and money because it's destined to fail. It really feels like I'm doing something wrong. I know that therapy is helpful for a lot of people. Why can't it be helpful for me?*

(This client had actually been able to identify some small but steady gains in therapy with her new therapist, but the emotional flashback leaves her doubting, unable to feel good about her decisions.)

- *(Pause) Three Deep Breaths*
- *Check-In:*

  COACH *Offers compassion.*

(Notice the feelings of confusion, powerlessness, and bigness of problem. This is an indication that you are having an emotional flashback. Know that Coach can be called upon for support in attending to the emotional realm.)

- Big feelings there. Notice them.
- Notice the feeling of worried. Worrying is a signal for you to slow down and be with yourself. Minimize distractions.
- Assure TVP that you are committed to getting the emotional support you need.
- Remind yourself that any important decision can wait until you are calm and grounded. Allow things to settle and fall into place. It's okay to not know the answer for a while.
- If possible, find a soft blanket, wrap yourself in it, and put yourself down for a nap.
- Notice that you are comparing, and remove comparisons from the equation (*Therapy is helpful for them, not me*).
- Identify any early angers and tender vulnerable emotions.
  - ✓ Resentment
  - ✓ Blaming
  - ✓ Judging
  - ✓ Comparing
  - ✓ Fear
  - ✓ Grief
  - ✓ Vulnerability
- With Coach's support your nervous system begins to calm down so that you can then check with Challenger to see what is real. If your nervous system is too

- aroused and you are in an emotional flashback, engaging in further analysis can take you deeper into the flashback.
- Possibly reach out to someone you trust (talking to someone trusted and being listened to helps calm your nervous system).
- Notice what feels right or approaching right (Reach for gratitude for that).
- Notice the fear. Know that Coach is available to hold you while you safely breathe through the sensations. Your feelings are neither right nor wrong. It's okay just to notice your fear and do nothing for right now.

CHALLENGER *Provides safety and structure, Allies with Coach, and Supports accountability, growth and next steps.*

Once you feel a bit calmer, check in with Challenger.

- Remind your TVP that your intention is to grow and expand your emotional development/maturity while ensuring safety.
- There is so much you can learn from this situation, and the feelings you are experiencing. Underneath all of this angst, see if you can recognize the overwhelm and terror around being on your own and unsupported in the past during such a difficult time.
- Worrying, ruminating, blaming yourself and awfulizing was a strategy you used when you were a teenager at home and you didn't have the support you needed. Rather than feel all the overwhelming feelings of loss and grief and terror, you developed highly analytical defenses that kept you disconnected from your feelings and occupied your mind. You were a teenager then, and in many ways you were still a child. You have developed and changed in many ways, and so have your circumstances.
- Gratitude for the ingenuity of this strategy that you have used in the past to protect you from intolerable emotions; gratitude for your bright, nuanced, imaginative mind. Appreciation that you have survived this difficult time.
- Assure TVP that you will remain alert to any evidence of real problems that could be making this therapeutic situation unsafe, or truly a bad fit.
- What is left when you remove abuse (blame, shame, comparing) from this equation?
- Challenger helps to cut through the confusion by offering frameworks and questions to determine whether there is something you can do to be accountable and learn from the past, which could include:
  - ✓ Identifying differences between what was true then and what is true now.
  - ✓ Opening to new information that can help you distinguish fact from fiction.
  - ✓ Recognizing the errors in logic you have picked up along the way and making appropriate adjustments.
  - ✓ Forgiving yourself for past mistakes.

- Write down the repetitive thoughts and ruminations you have been having.
- What's the associated story that your adolescent self would like us to know? It's safe to allow yourself to know what happened, and connect with the pain. Coach can be called upon for support with emotions, compassion and release.
- Ask for very clear and unambiguous signals from your guides/Nature/Spirit/your Highest Self. Then allow yourself to be guided (put the analysis down - relax).
- Give yourself a specific time in which you will re-visit the question *(Make a decision to "not decide" about the therapist until X time.)*
- Keep showing up for appointments with your therapist until you get unambiguous guidance that it is no longer a good choice for you (until you get literally pushed into the answer to your question, and a clear knowing).
- Allow your therapist to be your guide during sessions. Follow her without abandoning yourself. Think of it as dancing. She leads. Your role is to follow and notice what you like and don't like about this process. She is the professional. She is your guide. But therapy is *for* you. See what you can learn from her. She doesn't have all your answers but she has some. And this relationship you are building with her over time will give you another working model of:
  - ✓ What you like.
  - ✓ What you don't like.
  - ✓ What works for you.
  - ✓ What doesn't work for you.
  - ✓ Receiving new information on what it feels like to receive/allow and to be supported well.

CREATOR *(Tells me about my feelings and needs)*

3. Shift focus to something other than the urge (Focused Attention) for 10-20 minutes.

(Check-in can happen in any order. Creator tells you about how you are feeling right now, which is likely to feel some better after having spent some time with Coach and Challenger.)

Spend 10-20 minutes doing a focused attention activity. In this case, the *TET Holding Position* or journaling would help the body make the shifts that have been initiated by check-in with Coach and Challenger, and help support the client in resisting any urge to return to compulsive rumination and worry.

3) (Pause) Body Scan

4) How would I like this to go differently in the future?

In the future I imagine myself clear and grounded. I would like to be able to clearly recognize any progress I am making with my therapist, and to also be able to trust that the progress I am seeking may not be immediately evident. I would like to be able to trust that if I'm on the wrong track that I will have clear and unambiguous evidence that I need to make changes, and to do so with grace and ease. I would like to trust myself and feel worthy of high quality support, growth, and practical, measurable gains in my self-confidence, self-esteem, and ability to relax and benefit from the companionship of close and intimate others.

Module 6 Quiz 1:

1) Parenting involves:
   A. Maintaining a safe, age-appropriate home environment.
   B. Understanding some basics about child development.
   C. Staying connected even when your children are frightened, misbehaving or angry.
   D. Gaining the skills necessary to manage strong emotions and model healthy behaviors for your infants and children.
   E. Getting support when needed.
   F. Understanding that you need not be perfect to be good enough.
   G. All of the above.

2) The myelinated vagus allows higher mammals, including humans to:
   A. Relax in the presence of another higher mammal.
   B. Have positive affective experiences
   C. Engage socially with other beings
   D. Build relationships
   E. Experience spirituality
   F. All of the above

3) (True or False) For people who have not recovered from trauma (early relational trauma or single-incident trauma), the trust necessary to play and connect with others is something that becomes restored alongside body awareness and the ability to live in a relaxed body.

4) Which of the following are NOT true about both play and focused attention?
   A. They both promote the development of emotion regulation
   B. They are both avenues for exploring what is possible
   C. They both facilitate innovation
   D. Both are associated with relaxation of the body and mind
   E. They are both valuable modes of exploration
   F. None of the above

5) (True or False) Novelty is important aspect of focused attention because it helps stimulate curiosity.

Congratulations!

All of your efforts are paying off. Even the smallest of efforts – considering, imagining and fantasizing about what you desire – all pay off. Each baby step you make improves your ability to be a better parent to yourself. Get to know these basic tools and then step back, relax and watch your Inner Creator grow and thrive.

And if you EVER return to doubt (and you will), remember:

You have all the support you need.

You actually have a lot of skills and resources.

You never have to get it "perfect."

You can allow things to just happen sometimes.

Staying aware of how you feel will save you a lot of trouble in the long run.

Tending to the little things as you go along will keep you from reaching that point of overwhelm in the future.

Play.

Relax.

Toni Rahman, LCSW is a psychotherapist specializing in trauma and attachment. Her passions include Eastern and indigenous healing practices, psychology, spirituality and gender issues, as well as issues of social and economic justice. She is passionate about exploring ways to support others in making profound shifts in their life experience. She is a Trauma-Informed Care Practitioner, a Certified EMDR Practitioner and EMDRIA Approved Consultant, trained in CranioSacral Therapy & Somato-Emotional Release, Chinese Five Element Theory, Dream Interpretation, Quantum Touch and Energy Balancing. Toni now lives in Mexico, where she has a small private practice. She has been healing her own early relational trauma and growing as a therapist since 2004.

For more information, contact Toni at:

toniarahman@hotmail.com
US Number: (573) 999-6011
Mexico Number: 33 3447 5624
Visit her website/blog at tonirahman.com, beinginmybody.com or
Toni Rahman on Facebook

References

Beatty, M. *The Language of Letting Go*. New York: Hazeldon Foundation, 1990.

Chapman, G & Thomas, J. *The Five Languages of Apology: How to Experience Healing in All Your Relationships*. Chicago: Northfield Publishing, 2006.

Foster, J. *The Courage to Love: Diving Into the Body*. ProducersPick Interview with Tami Simon at Sounds True March 2017.

Gawain, Shakti. *Creative Visualization. The Power of Your Imagination to Create What You Want In Your Life*. Novato: Nataraj Publishing, 2002.

Hicks, Esther & Jerry. *Ask and It Is Given: Learning to Manifest Your Desires*. Carlsbad: Hay House, Inc. 2004.

Karen, R. *Becoming Attached: First Relationships and How They Shape Our Capacity to Love*. New York: Oxford University Press, 1994.

Leu, L. *NonViolent Communication Workbook: A Practical Guide for Individual, Group, or Classroom Study*. Encinitas: Puddledancer Press, 2003.

Levine, A. & Heller, Rachel S. F. *Attached: The New Science of Adult Attachment And How It Can Help You Find – And Keep – Love*. New York: Penguin Group, 2010.

Lipton, B. *The Biology of Belief: Unleashing the Power of Consciousness, Matter & Miracles*. Hay House, 2008.

Porges, S.W. (2001). *The Polyvagal Theory: Phylogenetic Substrates of a Social Nervous System*. Internal Journal of Psychophysiology.

Rahman, T. *Being In My Body: What You Might Not Have Known About Trauma, Dissociation & The Brain*. Columbia: Open Sesame Publishing, 2016.

Rosenberg, M.B. *NonViolent Communication: A Language of Compassion*. Encinitas: Puddledancer Press, 2000.

Roth, G. *Maps to Ecstasy: A Healing Journey for the Untamed Spirit*. Novato: Nataraj Publishing, 1998.

Schwartz, R.C. *Internal Family Systems*. New York: The Guilford Press, 1995.

Siegel, D.J. *Aware: The Science and Practice of Presence*. New York: TarcherPerigee, 2018.

Tatkin, S. *Wired for Love: How Understanding Your Partner's Brain and Attachment Style Can Help You Defuse Conflict and Build a Secure Relationship*. Oakland: New Harbinger Publications, Inc. 2001.

Tipping, C.C. *Radical Forgiveness: A Revolutionary Five-Stage Process to Heal Relationships, Let Go of Anger and Blame & Find Peace in Any Situation*. Boulder: Sounds True, Inc., 2002.

Van der Kolk, Bessel. *The Body Keeps the Score: Brain, Mind, and Body In the Healing of Trauma*. New York: Penguin Books, 2014.

Walker, Pete. *Complex PTSD: From Surviving to Thriving: A Guide and Map for Recovering from Childhood Trauma*. Self Published, 2013.

Weinhold, B. & Weinhold, J. *Developmental Trauma: The Game Changer in the Mental Health Profession*. Colorado Springs: CICRCL Press, 2015.

Weinhold, B. & Weinhold, J. *How to Break Free of the Drama Triangle & Victim Consciousness*. Colorado Springs: CICRCL Press, 2016.

Other Resources

Adult Children of Alcoholics
     https://adultchildren.org/
Al-Anon
     https://al-anon.org/
Alsana Treatment Center for Eating Disorders
     https://www.alsana.com/
Betty Martin – Wheel of Consent
     https://bettymartin.org/
Colorado Professional Development Center
     https://coprofdevcenter.org/
David Deida
     https://deida.info/
Interview with Stephen Porges – Dharma Cafe
     https://www.youtube.com/watch?v=8tz146HQotY
Janel Mirendah, Baby Keeper/Listener – Doula
     Facebook: The Other Side of the Glass
Mary Cruise Healing Arts (Tai Chi)
     http://marycruisehealingarts.com/tai-chi/
Shaking to Release Psoas and calm the Nervous System
     https://www.youtube.com/watch?v=Y3x_ITdzKbI#t=47.466957
Somatic Movement Blog
     https://thesomaticmovement.wordpress.com/
Stephen Karpman – Originator of the Drama Triangle
     https://karpmandramatriangle.com/
Stuart Brown - Play
     https://www.ted.com/talks/stuart_brown_says_play_is_more_than_fun_it_s_vital
The Drama Triangle PowerPoint
     https://www.slideshare.net/marva78/the-drama-triangle

Pre-Test & Quiz Answers:

Pre-Test:

1) D
2) False (Trauma is the body's response to extreme stress. Not having basic needs for safety and attunement constitute trauma when an individual is vulnerable and can't meet his or her own needs.)
3) C
4) True (You win the game when you win "Victim" status. However, you lose authenticity, interpersonal safety and any hope for real intimacy. You must be *willing* to ask for what you want 100% of the time, whether you actually ask for it or not.)
5) A

Module 1 Quiz 1:

1) True
2) D
3) A

Module 1 Quiz 2:

1) E
2) E
3) True
4) D
5) E

Module 2 Quiz 1:

1) True
2) B
3) C
4) E

Module 3 Quiz 1:

1) True
2) E
3) F
4) D

Module 4 Quiz 1:

1) E
2) True
3) F
4) E
5) C (Love allows the expression of all emotions, not just "positive" ones.)

Module 5 Quiz 1:

1) F (If you hear yourself complaining it is probably time to check and see how you are blocking legitimate solutions due to rigidity and fear or ignoring or denying important feelings and needs. Hopelessness can also be an automatic response to stress.)
2) F
3) D
4) True
5) E

Module 6 Quiz 1:

1) G
2) F
3) True
4) F (They're all correct!!! Go and focus your attention until you connect with the playful nature of your inner Creator!)
5) True